YAO HSIN-NUNG was born in Fukien in 1905. Schooled in both the Confucian tradition and in 'Western learning', he began to write plays while at Soochow University. In 1931 Yao became editor of the World Book Company in Shanghai. Five years later he joined the Board of Editors of *T'ien Hsia Monthly* and became vice-chairman of the scenario-committee of the Star Motion Picture Company. In August, 1937, Yao was sent as China's delegate to the Fifth Soviet Theatre Festival and to the International P.E.N. Conference in London, where he was invited to talk on Chinese poetry at Alexandra Palace, so becoming the first Chinese to appear on television. In 1938 he was granted a research fellowship in Western drama at Yale and, returning to China in 1940, was offered the chair of drama at Futan University. In 1941, as producer-manager of T'ien Fêng Theatre in Shanghai, Yao wrote *Ch'ing-kung Yuan* (The Malice of Empire) and founded the famous K'u Kan Players.

In 1948 Yao left mainland China and joined the Yung Hwa Studio in Hong Kong. There in 1949 he adapted *Ch'ing-kung Yuan* as a film entitled *The Sorrows of the Forbidden City*. In 1950 the film became the subject of a serious controversy between Mao Tse-tung and Liu Shao-chi, described as 'the first important struggle on the cultural and ideological front in liberated China'.

From 1952 to 1959 Yao was editor of the South Wind Publishing Company and, after joining the United College of the Chinese University, Hong Kong, became Head of the Department of Chinese Language and Literature. He is currently Visiting Professor of Chinese at the University of Hawaii.

The Malice of Empire

The Malice of Empire

BY YAO HSIN-NUNG

TRANSLATED AND WITH AN INTRODUCTION
BY JEREMY INGALLS

UNIVERSITY OF CALIFORNIA PRESS
BERKELEY AND LOS ANGELES 1970

First published in the United States in 1970 by University of California
Press, Berkeley & Los Angeles, California

*No public performance of this play or any part of it may be presented unless
the permission of the publishers has first been granted in writing.*
*All enquiries regarding performing rights (professional and amateur) should
be addressed to the Subsidiary Rights Department, University of California
Press, Berkeley, California 94720, U.S.A.*
*Permission to make minor cuts or modifications of the text of the play for
stage, radio or television production will be granted by the publishers. Major
cuts or modifications will be referred by the publishers to the author or
translator.*

PRINTED IN GREAT BRITAIN

Foreword

Translation of Yao Hsin-nung's *Ch'ing-kung Yüan* began in 1958 as a collaborative venture suggested by Dr S. Y. Teng. Concurrently engaged, however, in research and translations more immediately germane to his specialities in political history, Dr Teng, in 1961, encouraged me to take over the making of an English translation of Yao's play. The translation here presented is entirely my own; and for it Dr Teng should bear no responsibility. But I continue to be grateful to him for calling my attention to the play and for his advice and assistance from 1958 to 1961.

Since 1961 I have been in continuous correspondence with Yao Hsin-nung, who resides in Hong Kong. I am grateful to him for the play itself. Our reasons for calling the play, in English, *The Malice of Empire* are detailed in my 'Introduction', which follows here. Yao Hsin-nung has also generously assisted me with information regarding the history of performances of the play and of its later cinema version, for which in 1948 he wrote the film-script. For his cordial support and approval of my English rendering of his play, I am sincerely appreciative. Though in 1964 he published in Hong Kong a shortened Chinese version, we have agreed that, for both the literary and historical record, we should present in English my translation of the original, uncut Chinese text known to Chinese theatre-goers ever since 1941.

I also express thanks to Drs Cyril Birch, Shih-hsiang Chen, L. Carrington Goodrich, J. Robert Hightower, Teruko Kachi, Dearing Lewis, Alfred Marks, Johanna Menzel Meskill, and Chester C. I. Wang for their several courtesies pertinent to the completion of this translation.

JEREMY INGALLS

174072

Contents

Introduction

Yao Hsin-nung's play: its literary pertinence

In *Ch'ing-kung Yüan* Yao Hsin-nung has created a work of durable literary merit. What is essential in this play, as in any successful dramatic work, is the action itself: the individualizing voice and point of view defining each of the characters; the selection of moments of encounter and consequence; the deployment of tensions accessible to the audience; the soundly projected insights into human nature. In these terms, even apart from the perennial significance of its theme, Yao's play is an intrinsically convincing literary achievement.

Its action set within the Ch'ing dynasty palaces in Peking at the end of the nineteenth century, the play takes its dynamic from a triangle of conflicting temperaments. In the power duel between the Manchu Empress Dowager and the Emperor's concubine, Lady Chên, the Emperor becomes, from several aspects, the victim of both these women. The play's central tension ensues from the Dowager's recognition that the major threat to her autonomy springs not from her nephew, the Emperor, nor from the men he may gather around him, but pre-eminently from Lady Chên. This girl might easily begin to climb the ladder from imperial concubine to regent of the Empire by the same rungs that the Empress Dowager herself had used.

The play's structural effectiveness derives from Yao's perception that the Dowager's seeming triumph over Lady Chên becomes itself an index to the crumbling power of the Ch'ing dynasty. In the final scene, Lady Chên's last summons to the Emperor, the steady voice echoing from the brink of the well in the Empress Dowager's courtyard, merges with the artillery barrage on Peking. Yao visualizes the oncoming collapse of the Empress Dowager's regime as a fatality inherent in the Dowager's own despotic drive to destroy those within her court who might have been her most effective successors.

THE MALICE OF EMPIRE

For Western readers and audiences who are curious about Chinese history, the play has an immediate value since Yao's interpretation of character is historically sound and defensible. His imaginative presentation of events which take place in the Manchu palaces during the period of the Emperor's attempted government reforms, on through the *coup d'état* to the Boxer uprising and the fall of Peking, is based upon documented evidence. The Dowager was indeed a termagant. The eunuch, Li Lien-ying, was her vicious sycophant. Yüan Shih-k'ai did betray the Emperor. The Emperor was both earnest and timid. The Manchu princes did connive with the Boxers. The Dowager's personal extravagances and Li Lien-ying's graft were also real factors in the crisis for China at the end of the nineteenth century. Lady Chên was the special target of the Dowager's ill will. But though the play is rooted in these historical authenticities, it is much more than a documentary tale.

For historians of the theatre, Yao's play is an example of a characteristic development in Asian theatre during the twentieth century: the move from the special characteristics of national theatre towards what is now called, appropriately, international theatre. In China, this has meant a move away from the picaresque sequences of the operatic tale. *Ch'ing-kung Yüan* aptly reflects the point made by Earle Ernst of the University of Hawaii in his 'The Case for Oriental-Western Theatre Study'[1] regarding the convergence of themes and theatre techniques in the twentieth century around the world. But beyond its relevance both as a history play and as a datum in theatre history, the enduring power of *Ch'ing-kung Yüan* resides in factors which always distinguish major dramatic compositions: a perennially significant theme realized through characters whose vigour and verisimilitude carry them to an enduring life within the imagination of a world audience.

The literary strength of *Ch'ing-kung Yüan* is confirmed in the play's capacity to make history as well as to reflect it. The following chronological survey of the public career of the play and its subsequent opera and film versions is based upon personal correspondence with the author as well as upon articles appearing in mainland China and in Hong Kong newspapers and journals.[2]

---

[1] See *The Yearbook of Comparative and General Literature*, No. 11, 1962, pp. 177–82.
[2] A compendium of pertinent publications in Chinese can be found in the May, 1967, issue of the Hong Kong monthly magazine, *Ming Pao* (Volume II, No. 5). Included are

Yao's play and the film version of Yao's play; 1941 to 1967

The debut of *Ch'ing-kung Yüan*, in Shanghai on July 15, 1941, preceded by three years that of Jean Anouilh's *Antigone*. Some members of the Paris audience for Anouilh's *Antigone* celebrated his version of the old Greek tale as a pro-Vichy drama. A larger audience, however, equated the young heroine's struggle against despotic rule with French resistance to German Occupation forces. Yao Hsin-nung's play, on its opening night and thereafter, stirred analogous arguments among Chinese theatre-goers.

Most understood correctly enough that this story of the struggle of Lady Chên against the Empress Dowager and on behalf of the young Manchu Emperor's effort at government reform functioned, on the Chinese stage, as an indictment directed against authoritarianism still formidable in twentieth-century China. But some regarded the play solely as an attack upon the Japanese. By the summer of 1941 the resistance to Japanese Occupation forces in China had of course already become acute. Others interpreted the play as an attack upon Chiang Kai-shek. Still others regarded it as an attack upon Mao Tse-tung. On into the 1960's, Chinese have continued to debate these competing interpretations. But the play's target, as Yao Hsin-nung affirms, is tyranny itself, despotism in all its guises.

In 1942 the play opened in Tientsin. After its first night, the commander of Japanese Occupation forces in North China banned the play. The published reason for the ban mentioned the lines referring to the Sino-Japanese war of 1894–95. But Japan had won that war, a fact which the play's mention of this war also makes clear. It is more likely that the Japanese commander recognized the force of the play as a challenge to despotism and regarded it as a literary assault upon the Japanese Occupation and an affront to the Japanese Emperor. Though the Japanese ban closed the play, this did not directly affect Yao himself, who was then still in Shanghai. He had had no connection with the Tientsin presentation of *Ch'ing-kung Yüan*, a venture undertaken by a North Chinese troupe using pirated copies. But along with bankrupting the sanguine

articles by mainland Communist critics, statements by Mao Tse-tung relevant to the film version of Yao's play, portions of the film-script showing alterations introduced by the film's producer, Li Tsu-yung, and the film's director, Chu Shih-lin, as well as Yao Hsin-nung's own comments upon the controversy surrounding the play and the film.

Tientsin theatre manager, the ban precluded all further production of the play in Japanese occupied areas. After the defeat of Japan in World War II, Yao's play was revived in several major Chinese cities and again drew large audiences.

In 1948, Li Tsu-yung of the Hong Kong Yung Hwa Motion Picture Company commissioned Yao Hsin-nung to write a script for a cinema adaptation of the play. The film version, titled *Ching-kung Mi-shih, Inside Story of the Ch'ing Palaces*, was shown in urban centres throughout China and, in 1949, received the Best Film Award of the Chinese Press Association. In the film, although Yao's own scenario had for the most part been followed, the film's director, Chu Shih-lin, introduced several scenes of his own invention and, at the urging of the film's producer, Li Tsu-yung, devised, for the film's closing scenes, an ending markedly different from that in Yao's play and Yao's own film-script. These changes introduced by Chu Shih-lin and Li Tsu-yung unwittingly con-tributed to the subsequent condemnation of the film as 'reactionary' in the years following the ascendancy of the Maoist regime in mainland China.

The first noticeable pressures from Peking under Mao Tse-tung appeared, however, to be directed primarily against Yao's stage-play. These pressures from 1949 to 1953 forced the Shanghai publisher of the play-text finally to withdraw all bookstore copies from circulation. All major city theatre troupes officially dropped the play from their repertoires. But some troupes continued to perform it, advertising it as an 'old' play by an 'anonymous' author and pre-senting it sometimes in Mandarin and sometimes in local dialects.

In 1954 the stage play began to be presented as a Chinese opera. Again Yao Hsin-nung's name was never mentioned and, now resident in Hong Kong since 1948, he received no financial com-pensation for the use of his work. In Shao Hsing opera style the play was given its first operatic performances, before overflow audiences, at the Shanghai Yüeh Chu Theatre. The opera company made no major alteration of Yao's text but gave it a new title, 'Emperor Kuang Hsü and the Pearl Concubine.' From 1954 to 1957, city theatres, including those in Shanghai, Nanking, and Hangchow, presented the play in various local opera styles. In 1957, just before the end of the 'let the hundred flowers bloom' period, and during Liu Shao-ch'i's ascendancy, the stage play itself was reinstated, placed upon an officially recommended list of 'exemplary plays', and openly performed in Peking. In 1958, however, *Ch'ing-kung Yüan*, along with several others among the 'exemplary plays', was again forbidden. Even so, opera versions continued to be staged. Yao has reported to me, from information transmitted to him in Hong Kong, that an opera adaptation called 'Pearl Concubine' was performed in Peking as late as 1962 'right under Mao's nose'. But from the onset of Mao's 'Great Cultural Revolution' in 1963 the prohibition against *Ch'ing-kung Yüan* and all of its adaptations was thoroughly enforced throughout mainland China.

The film version of the play has experienced a similar history. Officially it was not shown in Communist China between the end of 1950 and the spring of 1967, and the film reels, seized in 1949, remained presumably under the control of the film department within the propaganda bureau. But the host of condemnatory essays directed against *Ch'ing-kung Mi-shih* during the spring of 1967 suggest that, whether or not the film was occasionally shown during the intervening years, its popularity between 1948 and 1950 had never been forgotten.

In 1950, Lu Ting-i, Chou Yang, and Hu Ch'iao-mu, members of the Peking Film Supervising Board, had re-approved the distribution of *Ch'ing-kung Mi-shih* and it was shown all over China. This board belongs to the order of government departments that was, at this time, under the direction of Liu Shao-ch'i. Liu himself is reputed to have consistently regarded *Ch'ing-kung Mi-shih* as both a good film and a 'patriotic' one. It is reported, however, that Mao Tse-tung personally ordered Liu to cease permitting the showing of the film. It was allowed no official circulation after 1950.

In a letter addressed to the Chinese Communist Party Central Committee on October 16, 1954, Mao denounced *Ch'ing-kung Mi-shih* as a work of 'treason'. By implication, everyone associated with the film now came within the category of 'traitor'. The denunciation potentially applied not only to the writer, Yao Hsin-nung, the producer, Li Tsu-yung, the director, Chu Shih-lin, and all members of the cast of the motion picture, but also to the official censors, Lu Ting-i, Chou Yang, and Hu Chiao-mu. The phrasing of Mao's letter could also implicate Liu Shao-ch'i; and Liu, as a member of the Central Committee, can be assumed to have had knowledge of the letter's content. But the existence of this 1954 denunciation did not come to public knowledge until January 3, 1967.

On that date Yao Wen-yüan, a spokesman for Mao Tse-tung, published in the official Peking newspaper, the *People's Daily*, an article, entitled 'Rebuking the Anti-Revolutionary Two-Faced Chou Yang", which included references to Mao's letter of 1954. That the article is only incidentally concerned with Chou Yang himself is patent in the article's context as well as its content. By January of 1967 Chou Yang had already not only been under attack for months but had long since been dismissed from his major appointments, including his former post as deputy chief of propaganda.[1] Yao Wen-yüan's article, mentioning the film version of Yao's play and condemning those associated with its direction and distribution, has an unstated but readily discernible target. Its remarks on 'revisionism' and upon 'two-faced' individuals within the Party are aimed primarily at Liu Shao-ch'i.

That Liu Shao-ch'i was the intended target became explicit on March 30, 1967, in *Red Flag*, major journal of official Chinese Communist doctrine. This issue of *Red Flag* carried the article, 'Patriotism or National Betrayal? The Reactionary Film, *Ch'ing-kung Mi-shih*.' The article's author, Chi Pen-yu, criticizes the film's interpretation of events in late nineteenth-century China. In a brief paragraph Chi denounces Yao Hsin-nung. After calling him a 'reactionary scribbler', a servant of 'British-American imperialism and the comprador-bourgeoisie', and a 'minor running-dog of the reactionary ruling classes', Chi makes what seems intended to be the maximum charge against Yao Hsin-nung, that he 'escaped to Hong Kong'.

Chi's article leaves no doubt that the chief individual on target is Liu Shao-ch'i. Identified as the 'top Party person in authority taking the capitalist road', Liu is accused of having praised the film, *Ch'ing-kung Mi-shih*, as 'patriotic'. His having expressed this opinion is cited as evidence of Liu's support of 'imperialism, feudalism, and the reactionary bourgeoisie'. The matter of the film then disappears as Chi, through several paragraphs, berates Liu on such counts as favouring concessions to private industry and the allowance of some amount of private property to peasants. Chi then

---

[1] See, for an excellent report and analysis of the case of Chou Yang, Merle Goldman's 'The Fall of Chou Yang,' *The China Quarterly*, Number 27, July–September, 1967.

brings in the culminating charge, that Liu 'wildly' opposes 'the great leader, Chairman Mao, and the great thought of Mao Tse-tung'.

This *Red Flag* article received coverage in all mainland Chinese newspapers and all publications abroad controlled by Peking. During April and May, for example, mainland journals such as the *People's Daily*, *Kwang Ming Daily News*, *Liberation Army Daily News*, and Shanghai *Wen Hui Pao*, and Hong Kong newspapers such as *Ta Kung Pao*, *Wen Hui Pao*, and *Hsin Wan Pao* inveighed against Liu Shao-ch'i, against the film, *Ch'ing-kung Mi-shih*, and whoever could be associated with its production or approval. Typical of rhetorical invective is the title of an article by Lo Ssu-ting appearing in the May 19, 1967, edition of the Peking *People's Daily*: 'Coup d'etat and Anti-Coup d'etat Struggle under the Proletarian Dictatorship: Why Does the Biggest Clique-in-Power that Treads the Road of Capitalism Want to Protect the Reactionary Film, *Ch'ing-kung Mi-shih*?'

The drive to eradicate popular regard for *Ch'ing-kung Mi-shih* culminated in a public re-run of the film. On orders from Mao Tse-tung the populace throughout mainland China was summoned, from late May through June, 1967, to view it. At these showings, audiences were lectured at length on the film's 'treasonous revisionism'. These lectures, so far as can be learned, concentrated attack upon the same film sequences to which the earlier published articles also direct most attention. By irony of circumstances, these film scenes all happen to be ones that Yao did not compose, scenes inserted, during the filming in 1948, by the film director, Chu Shih-lin, and, in one instance, by the producer, Li Tsu-yung.

Chu Shih-lin's alterations included scenes plagiarized from other plays. Some of the scenes the director introduced were, it is true, extensions of events to which there are allusions within Yao's play. The Emperor's tutor, for example, who is given a passing mention in the play, appears in the film, in a scene in which he urges upon the Emperor the importance of winning the trust of the Chinese people. The defeat of the Chinese navy in the Sino-Japanese war comes on screen and also a sequence showing the escape of the Chinese reformist leader, K'ang Yu-wei. These, together with the film shots of Lady Chên praying for the well-being of China and of the rioting by the Boxers, were all introduced by Chu Shih-lin.

Yao had objected to the plagiarized scenes. He also deplored the anachronism created by insertion of twentieth-century popular songs. But he protested most strongly against the scenes inserted in the film's final reel. He had pointed out to both the director and the producer that the events shown in the closing sequence of *Ch'ing-kung Mi-shih* have no justification from history and falsify the intentions of both his stage play and his own film-script.

The closing scenes, composed jointly by Chu Shih-lin and Li Tsu-yung, show the flight of the Empress Dowager and the Emperor from Peking. History records that Manchu guards had cleared all country people from the escape route. But the final sequence in *Ch'ing-kung Mi-shih* shows the Emperor followed through the countryside by devoted peasants, who present gifts of food and echo the advice of the Emperor's tutor that the Emperor must find his strength among the common people. Yao's original film-script had ended as his play ends: stricken by the death of Lady Chên, the Emperor emerges alone from the Dowager's well yard. A tragic and not merely pathetic figure, his own vacillations, along with the Empress Dowager's self-absorbed arrogance, have contributed to the crisis now ensuing for the Manchu ruling family and for China. By contrast, the film's ending, invented by Chu and Li, implies that all the hazards of absolutism can be resolved simply by peasant loyalty to a new leader.

Yao remarks that he had objected to the film-script alterations as every author usually protests, in vain, the autocracy of film directors and producers. He had not recognized that Chu and Li, in inventing and insisting upon their own ending for the film, probably had specific political intentions in mind. Yao came to realize only in later years that Chu and Li probably intended the film to serve as a satire against Chiang Kai-shek and a means of currying favour with Mao Tse-tung. But it is obvious, Yao adds, that, whatever their intentions, neither Chu Shih-lin nor Li Tsu-yung, in 1948, could have foreseen that film sequences they had introduced into *Ch'ing-kung Mi-shih* would be singled out during faction fights within the Chinese Communist Party.

Maoist criticism directed at the film's final sequence castigates the scenes depicting peasants offering gifts to the Emperor. Such scenes, Maoist critics say, imply that peasants fawned upon the Manchus and prove the film's intent to demean the Chinese populace. The critics interpret the peasants' speeches to the Emperor, urging him to depend upon the common people, as an intended insult to Mao Tse-tung.

Chi Pen-yu develops a charge against the film also made by the Maoist critic, Yao Wen-yuan, inveighing against the film's presentation of the Boxers. The Boxers have no stage role in Yao Hsin-nung's play, but allusions to them in connection with events off-stage in Act IV, comments by the Emperor, Lady Chên, and Liu San-erh, deplore Boxer rioting and its encouragement by some of the Manchus, including the Empress Dowager. In the film, the Boxer sequence, introduced by the director, Chu Shih-lin, registers the Boxers' attachment to magic practices and amulets and their frenetic assaults upon foreigners. Never mentioning the existence of Yao's play but holding him wholly accountable for the film, Chi Pen-yu, stressing Mao's dictum that the Boxer movement was an exemplary early phase of the People's Revolution, accuses Yao Hsin-nung of distorting history. In the May, 1967, issue of the Hong Kong *Ming Pao*, Yao replies that, though the Boxers' resentment of foreign domination is understandable, they lacked competent leadership and were defeated by their own superstitions and by their indiscriminate violence.

In *Ch'ing-kung Mi-shih* the Boxer sequence runs for less than five minutes. The many paragraphs devoted to it by the Maoist critics, however, would create the impression that the Boxer Rebellion is the chief subject of the film. Chi Pen-yu sees national betrayal in the fact that the film does not present the Boxers as its heroes. The Red Lanterns, the women's military brigades associated with the Boxers, have no part in the film. But Chi Pen-yu, speaking for Mao Tse-tung and Mao's wife, Chiang Ch'ing, further condemns the film for not presenting the women of the Red Lantern brigades as its heroines.

Maoist critics avoid discussing the role of the Empress Dowager and that of her niece, the Empress, who abets the Dowager in their mutual harassment of the Emperor and Lady Chên. The critics also avoid discussing the Dowager's other allies in her furtherance of despotism, the eunuch, Li Lien-ying, and the military commanders, Yuan Shih-k'ai and Jung-lu. From the Maoist viewpoint, the villains in the Ch'ing-kung, in the Manchu palaces, are Lady Chên and the Emperor. Chi Pen-yu asserts that Lady Chên is an 'imperialist agent'. In his lexicon, Lady Chên and the Emperor 'rely on imperialism': that is, they advocate Western concepts of government and favour representation from the Chinese bourgeoisie. Chi declares that *Ch'ing-kung Mi-shih* is a 'capitalist' film expressly designed to confuse the masses and to overthrow the dictatorship of the proletariat.

Another Maoist critic, Shih Hung-ping, asserts, in the *People's Daily*, that the figure of the Emperor is intended to represent Chiang Ching-kuo, the son of Chiang Kai-shek. Since the film was completed early in 1948, Shih Hung-ping might appear to be concerned with establishing a plausible chronology. Insistence by other critics that the figure of the Emperor was designed to represent Liu Shao-ch'i could raise questions as to how, even supposing a Liu Shao-ch'i faction had developed within the Chinese Communist Party as early as 1947–1948, a complete outsider such as the non-Communist Yao Hsin-nung could have known about it. But Shih Hung-ping's logic does not carry very far. The film was already in wide circulation during 1948. Chiang Kai-shek did not retreat to Taiwan until the spring of 1949. Nonetheless, Shih attacks the film as propaganda designed to aid the return of Chiang Kai-shek from Taiwan.

That already in 1941 Yao Hsin-nung stood apart from the partisans of Chiang Kai-shek as well as from the Chinese Communist Party is attested by his personal statements and by his life history. Since taking up residence in Hong Kong in 1948, Yao has repeatedly refused invitations to come to Taiwan as well as rejecting efforts by the Peking government to persuade him to return to the mainland.

However, identification of Yao Hsin-nung with either a Kuomintang cabal or a Liu Shao-ch'i cabal has, on the evidence, never been the controlling issue in the matter of the proscriptions either against Yao's play, *Ch'ing-kung Yüan*, or against its film version, *Ch'ing-kung Mi-shih*. From January through June, 1967, the film version was one further battlefield in the Maoist campaign against Liu Shao-ch'i. But major attempts to discourage interest in Yao's play preceded as well as accompanied procedures to discredit the film. As we have already noticed, copies of the play were withdrawn from circulation in mainland China and licensed productions of the play and even operatic adaptations had already disappeared from the stage by 1963.

Though from 1949 through 1967, propaganda attacks were also mounted against other plays and films,[1] one factor that may explain the particular animus against Yao's work is his memorable evocation of the ruthlessness and malice in the character of the Empress Dowager.

Informants in Hong Kong affirm, from sources on the mainland, that long before 1967 uncomplimentary remarks about Mao Tse-tung were current under the mask of comments on 'the Empress Dowager'. That such remarks had been current was also noted by at least one Hong Kong newspaper during the spring of 1967. Since both Yao's play and the film version were still popular and much discussed in 1949, when Mao Tse-tung himself became the new resident of the Ch'ing-kung, the old Manchu palaces, it is not impossible that Mao's immediate interest in closing the play and discouraging attention to the film reflected his own anticipation that comparisons linking him with the Dowager could be a threat to his public image.

With his attention to crowd psychology and familiarity with the habit among Chinese audiences of looking for political parables in old stories, he could very well be inclined to attempt to forestall or to control comparisons with a still well remembered earlier inhabitant of the Ch'ing-kung. That the issue involved the play much more than the person of the author, Yao Hsin-nung, is evident in the fact that, throughout the years of proscriptions against it, no issue was made of the person of the author, who was, in any event, not subject to the Peking government. That during the final campaign against the film version in 1967 there was a conscious intention to avoid bringing the play back into much public notice is also indicated in the fact that Chi Pen-yu's *Red Flag* article, the major propaganda piece, avoids mentioning that Yao Hsin-nung is a playwright or that it was his play, *Ch'ing-kung Yüan*, which occasioned the making of the film.

Together with the use of the film as an issue through which to continue the feud with Liu Shao-ch'i, the corollary issue appears to have been an intention finally to control the currency of com-

[1] A detailed study of the attack on Wu Han for his also popular history play, *The Dismissal of Hai Jui*, is available in Stephen Uhalley Jr.'s 'The Cultural Revolution and the Attack on the "Three Family Village",' *The China Quarterly*, Number 27, July-September, 1967, pp. 149-161.

parisons between Mao Tse-tung and the Dowager. Though considerable attention was given in the Maoist press to the equation between the film version of the Emperor and Liu Shao-ch'i, equal attention was given to extolling the Boxers and the Red Lanterns. This attention has been most often interpreted as solely part of the general campaign to build up the image of the Boxers and Red Lanterns as predecessors of Mao's Red Guards. But this emphasis also allowed a re-interpretation of the Empress Dowager, focusing attention on her function, scarcely mentioned in the play and only incidentally indicated in the film, as the supporter of the street brigades in their campaign against foreigners.

By publicizing finally in 1967, his treason charge initially placed before the Chinese Communist Party Central Committee in 1954, Mao Tse-tung accomplished two purposes. The phrasing of the treason charge, constantly set out in the newspapers and repeated again to the audiences required to attend the showing of the film in May and June, 1967, did threaten with a treason conviction anyone who expressed approval of the figure of the Emperor – that is, by equation, Liu Shao-ch'i – and his 'revisionism'. At the same time, it also became an act subject to treason charges to express any disapproval of the Empress Dowager – that is, by equation, Mao Tse-tung. In the Maoist version of history, the Dowager is to be considered a virtuous figure not only suppressing the 'revisionism' of Lady Chên and the Emperor but also inspiring and encouraging the revolutionary Boxers and Red Lanterns.

On the part of the Maoist critics and columnists the noticeably scant and inconsistent attention to Yao Hsin-nung himself during the 1967 campaign against the film version of the play suggests to me that Peking may have initially intended to use Chu Shih-lin, the director of the film, rather than Yao Hsin-nung, as the decoy figure in the scheduled procedures for 1967 to continue the polemics against Liu Shao-ch'i and to publicize the treason charge against whoever approved of the Emperor and disapproved of the Dowager. From a Maoist viewpoint Chu Shih-lin would have been directly vulnerable. It was he who created the scenes, not present in the play, around which the 1967 campaign was developed. Furthermore, since 1949, Chu had become the leader of a pro-Peking faction in Hong Kong and was probably directly subject to Chinese Communist Party discipline. Chu Shih-lin, however, died unexpectedly of a heart attack during the first week of January, 1967, in Hong Kong. The film's producer, Li Tsu-yung, had passed away seven years earlier. There is considerable indication that the name of Yao Hsin-nung was finally brought in, late in March, 1967, as the one possible surviving target, even though he did not very handily fit the standard pattern for a Maoist cultural revolution campaign.

One of the consequences of Peking's decision to bring Yao Hsin-nung's name into the 1967 campaign was an added interest on the part of the international press. It was an innovation, and accordingly news that a literary man who was neither a Communist nor a resident of mainland China subject to Peking should be made even a secondary target in an otherwise now familiar staging for Communist faction fights. Along with requests for interviews and articles for publication in other parts of Asia and in Europe as well as in Hong Kong, Yao was asked to broadcast on *Voice of America*. In this Chinese-language interview, April 7, 1967, beamed into mainland China, Yao again stressed that, in composing the play in 1941, he regarded the Japanese invaders and both Mao Tse-tung and Chiang Kai-shek as representative of types of authoritarianism but that his controlling concern was the creation of a theatre piece that could both dramatize and symbolize absolutism and authoritarianism whatever their sources and local manifestations. He commented, in closing, that so long as anyone, even though only privately, disagrees with Mao Tse-tung, the play is still serving within its intended function.

'Ch'ing-kung Yüan' and the biography of Yao Hsin-nung

Yao Hsin-nung's insights, expressed in the composition of *Ch'ing-kung Yüan*, into the characteristics of despotism and the character of despots did not spring from any traumatic personal confrontation with despotism. As is true of a number of major literary works, *Ch'ing-kung Yüan* is an objective projection, with appropriate historical resources, of the talents and insights of a writer steadily observing the shapes of events in his own nation in his own time and also observing both parallels and contrasts in the literature, history, and current politics of the world in general. He was in his thirty-sixth year when he wrote *Ch'ing-kung Yüan*.

By then he was well read in Chinese literature and history and familiar with several other literatures. By then he had experienced the process of Chinese revolutions from the death of the Empress Dowager during his early childhood to the concurrent warlord rivalries and the struggles between Yuan Shih-k'ai and Sun Yat-sen, to the polarizations in which Chinese aspirations for representative government were constantly under attrition from a hardening Kuomintang and a hardening Chinese Communism, up to the compounded crisis in Japan's invasion of China. By his thirty-sixth year he had also been abroad, in the Soviet Union, in Great Britain, and in the United States. Furthermore, Shanghai, the city he knew best, was, when he settled there again in 1940, still a cosmopolis.

Born in 1905, the son of a Fellow of the Hanlin Academy who was also, in the last years of the Ch'ing dynasty, commissioner of education for Fukien, Yao Hsin-nung had his elementary schooling in the classical Confucian tradition. After his father's death in 1913, Yao was schooled also in 'Western learning'. But he combined his Western studies with an enthusiasm for school plays in Chinese traditional style and became a devoted follower of Professor Wu Mei, an authority on Chinese classical drama. Going on to Soochow University and reading towards a degree in comparative international law, Yao still did not relinquish his interest in theatre. He wrote and produced, for campus drama groups, plays influenced by Western styles in scripts and staging. He eventually transferred to the university department of Chinese literature, from which he took his degree in 1931.

The composition and production, ten years later, of *Ch'ing-kung Yüan* marked him as a major talent in the new international style of Chinese theatre. But Yao's multiple careers began immediately on completion of his university degree. At twenty-six he was already on the Board of Editors of the World Book Company, Shanghai. At thirty-one he was deputy chairman of the film-script department for China's largest motion picture company, Shanghai's Star Motion Pictures. When he was thirty-two, he was sent as official representative from the Chinese government of Chiang Kai-shek to the Fifth Soviet theatre Festival in Moscow. From Russia he proceeded to England. There he made a lecture tour and, while in London representing China at the International P.E.N. Conference, was interviewed on BBC Television, the first Chinese, it is said, to have appeared on a television screen.

The next three years he spent in the United States. Supported by a Rockefeller Foundation grant, he studied radio programme techniques at the NBC studios and documentary film-making at the March-of-Time studio. He also took courses in the history of Western drama and dramatic composition at Yale University. He returned to Shanghai in 1940, completing *Ch'ing-kung Yüan* the following spring.

Continuing in mainland China until 1948 and subsequently in Hong Kong, Yao has produced both plays and films and has held several posts as a professor of dramatic literature. In addition to the composition of eleven film-scripts since 1940, he has also composed, along with *Ch'ing-kung Yüan*, twelve other stage plays. His *Hsi Shih* was produced at the 1956 Hong Kong Festival of the Arts. Successful productions of his *Ch'in Shih Huang Ti* and his *Lou Hsiang* marked the 1961 and 1962 theatre seasons in Hong Kong. Another recent play, *K'uai Lo Kuo*, a satire on totalitarianism in the guise of a children's play, has not thus far found a producer. In 1964, in his alternate role as a theatre entrepreneur, Yao produced in Hong Kong a version of Shakespeare's *The Merchant of Venice*, spoken in Cantonese and mounted in the style of Chinese classical theatre.

From 1940 to 1948 Yao held professorships on the faculties of Futan University, St John's University, and the Municipal Dramatic Academy in Shanghai. There he organized, with Huang Jo-lin and Wu Jen-shih, the celebrated Ku Kan Players. From 1948 to 1960 he lectured on Western and Chinese dramatic literature at several colleges and universities in Hong Kong. Since 1960 he has been on the faculty of the United College of the Chinese University, Hong Kong, and, from the spring of 1964 until his retirement in his sixty-second year served as Head of the department of Chinese language and literature. Affiliation of creative artists with universities is itself a characteristic twentieth-century development. This current phase in the biography of Yao Hsin-nung is one more aspect of his steady involvement in our world as it is.

His play, *Ch'ing-kung Yüan*, through its English translation and under its English title, *The Malice of Empire*, is now entering into circulation as an international theatre resource. Through circumstances no one could have foreseen in 1941, or even in 1949, Yao Hsin-nung found himself, because of matters related to the impact of *Ch'ing-kung Yüan* upon Chinese audiences, in the eye of a propaganda storm whirling from mainland China. But this contingent aspect in the history of *Ch'ing-kung Yüan* did not condition, just as it also did not create, the fact that, already long before 1967, Yao Hsin-nung, through both his work and his career, had earned a permanent place in the history of international theatre.

The purpose of the English title for 'Ch'ing-kung Yüan'

For a Chinese audience the title of Yao's play, *Ch'ing-kung Yüan*, reverberates with overtones and undertones that need no explanation. *Ch'ing-kung* connotes not solely the palace compounds dominating the capital city of Peking but the pressures of Manchu authoritarianism. In Chinese context, *Ch'ing-kung* itself prepares the title's key term, *yüan*: *bitterness, sorrow, malice*.

Literal English renderings of the title, however, whether as *Ch'ing Palace Malice* or *Manchu Palace Malice* or *Sorrows of the Ch'ing Palace*, ensue in either dastard cacophony or sentimental connotations inappropriate to the play's basic import. The force of *yüan*, with respect to the play's theme, is the *malice* of despotism.

The play dramatizes the malice of despotism through characters who, as Manchu dynasts, were responsible for ruling an empire. But Yao Hsin-nung's essential purpose has been to re-animate Ch'ing dynasty events in a dramatic work serving as a political parable. While already working, during the early 1960's, on the English translation of *Ch'ing-kung Yüan*, I was also trying to resolve a language problem I recognized in the play's Chinese title, inclusive of the fact that the term, *Ch'ing-kung*, whether in itself or in literal translations, lacks, for non-Chinese audiences, its immediately powerful Chinese connotations. When, in 1964, I suggested to Yao Hsin-nung that a viable English title conveying the play's basic import might be *The Malice of Empire*, he at once concurred.

Up to the closing days of March, 1967, neither Yao Hsin-nung nor I was aware of more than a few scattered reports, coming into Hong Kong since 1949, about proscriptions against his play and against its film version. These then seemed no more than the usual Chinese Communist proscriptions also directed against other plays and films, against more recent productions as well as such works as *Ch'ing-kung Yüan*, already current before Mao Tse-tung's arrival in Peking. That in 1967 Yao Hsin-nung suddenly found himself being maliciously attacked, in a campaign serving purposes solely of interest to Mao Tse-tung, reinforced, in ways unanticipated by either the author or the translator, the appropriateness of both the original title, *Ch'ing-kung Yüan*, and the English title, *The Malice of Empire*.

Yao Hsin-nung's play, in whatever language, is likely to retain both its dramatic impact and its symbolic pertinence. Varieties of imperial and imperious malice and its consequences in human history have never been, and are not likely to become, in any generation, exclusively characteristic of any one people or any one century.

Translating and editing

The English *The Malice of Empire* renders the original text of *Ch'ing-kung Yüan* in all its speaking parts and stage business. Slight turns or paraphrases in the translation of a few passages are an expected service by the translator to the author. Where over-literal translation produces, from the intransigency of languages, a false emphasis or misleading connotation, the collaboration of the translator with the author's general intention, rather than exercise-book literalism, seems the wise procedure.

Like every skilful playwright, Yao Hsin-nung establishes character partly through individual speech patterns, The translator's task, patently, is to transmit corresponding patterns. The loutish eunuch, T'ien Kuei-shou, for example, does not talk like the general, Jung-lu. And though the empress dowager might, in a romanticized tale, be accorded consistently formal speech modes, Yao, as a realist, has projected adroitly, in her speech patterns, her history as a social climber. When she reverts to gutter language, this is rendered in the English translation.

As to place-names, for most texts these are best left untranslated. In European context we are not usually conscious of the root-meaning of such place-names as *Vatican* or *Versailles*; where the place-name is solely a location pointer – *Ying-t'ai* or *Pei San-so* – such names, carried over into the English translation, sustain their Chinese aura. But with regard to the names of several of the halls and palaces in the Forbidden City, Yao Hsin-nung intends us to be aware of ironies implicit in these names with relation to events within the play which he assigns to these locales. Consequently, such names are given an English translation – as, for instance, Personal Harmony Hall – where, within the action of the play, the audience is invited to perceive that such harmony is ironically lacking.

As for personal names and titles – often a major problem in translations from Chinese – Yao's own procedures have largely eliminated the potential complexities. The empress dowager and the young emperor (posthumously, Tz'u-hsi and Kuang-hsü) are simply and conveniently *empress dowager* and *emperor*. The occasional variation, for the empress dowager, is the nickname which she accepted and regarded with favour, the address, *Old Buddha*. In his casting list, however, Yao identifies Kuang-hsü's empress as Lung-yü – which, in historical strictness, is not her 'name' during events prior to 1900. But since, within the text to be spoken, she is never addressed by this name, the English version omits this minor anachronism.

Early in the Chinese text Yao has the emperor address the dowager by a title which can be literally translated, Yao says, as 'begetter' or 'male parent'. Since even a Chinese audience, in the twentieth century, is unfamiliar with the term, Yao adds a footnote on this point, commenting that the dowager's partiality for this term reinforcing her 'emperor' role was one of her several idiosyncrasies. But for a non-Chinese-speaking audience, to hear so early in the play (and the term occurs only once and only at the opening of the prologue) a central figure addressed by a male title, among several male and female figures whose costuming is unfamiliar, can be unnecessarily confusing. For the English text this title is rendered *Imperial Parent*.

In the English text the imperial concubines are identified simply as *Chên* (approximate pronunciation, *Djŭn*) and her sister, *Chin* (Djin), omitting the identifying *fei – imperial concubine*. The action of the play itself makes explicit their appointment as concubines to the emperor. In direct address they are, in the English text, identified as *Lady Chên* and *Lady Chin*. This convention conveys more nearly the tone of respect involved than could be conveyed by having them addressed, in English, as *Concubine Chên* and *Concubine Chin*.

The titles provided for each scene of the play are Yao's own. Likewise, the frequent parenthetical instructions – *e.g.*, 'slyly', 'earnestly' – also all come from the original text. Even though it has seemed to the translator that the spoken text itself sufficiently implies these matters of tone and nuance, retention of these guides to interpretation is faithful to the playwright's style.

In translation nothing has been 'edited out'; for convenience in producing the play on stage, however, a few items have been 'edited in'. Besides the provision of a summary list of all persons of the play and of the time-and-place data at the beginning of the whole text (instead of solely at the opening of each of the several scenes), a few staging items have been added to those provided by the playwright: a needed exit area of which the Chinese description of the set gives no forewarning or an occasional needed further screen, table, or bench.

Production data at the opening of each scene is also sometimes given in order of convenience for easier visualization by the Western reader or producer rather than in the Chinese sentence-order of the original text. Again, however, no details are omitted.

In such editing the intention has been to serve the interests of the original composer by reducing barriers between the play and the English-speaking reader, performer, and producer. Cumbering the text with footnotes on such editing services would seem excessive since these minor items do not alter the play as heard and read but pertain only to convenience in stage performance.

Minor editing with respect to production details implies no criticism of the play as literature. The play as heard and read is the essential drama: the words and actions of characters evoking the encounters and tensions inherent to conflicts aggravated by the obsessive vanity of tyrants.

The Malice of Empire

Persons of the play

Nieh Pa-shih, elderly eunuch: Act I only.
Ts'ui Yu-kuei, eunuch, in his twenties: Acts II, III, IV.
Sun Te, eunuch: Act II.
Yuan Shih-k'ai, middle-aged administrator and army commander: Act II.
Jung-lu, high-ranking administrator and general, advisor to the dowager, now in his sixties: Act III.
Liu San-erh, boy eunuch: Acts III and IV.
T'ien Kuei-shou, loutish eunuch: Acts III and IV.
Ch'i, eunuch: Act IV.

WALK-ON ROLES:
Princess Ch'un (Fu-chin), in her fifties: Prologue only.
Elder Ta-hsing girl, about eighteen: Prologue only.
Younger Te-hsing girl, about seventeen: Prologue only.
Several ladies-in-waiting.
Several attendant eunuchs.
Two armed squadmen: Act IV only.

EDITOR'S NOTE: Directors will discover that, with costume and make-up changes, the play can be performed by a company of fifteen. For example, those playing the roles of Ch'un-yen and Ch'un-shou can double in the Prologue as the Teh-sing sisters and also serve later as tableau ladies-in-waiting; the Yuan Shih-k'ai actor in II might also play T'ien Kuei-shou, III and IV; the Jung-lu actor in III might play Ch'i in IV; the Sun Te actor in II might already have appeared as the walk-on Prince Ch'un in the Prologue; other doublings and triplings are possible. Though such procedure may not recommend itself for commercial production, it can be a valuable resource and extension of experience for small theatre workshop companies.

Time and place

Prologue

Time: winter of 1887.
Place: Personal Harmony Hall in the Old Palace, Peking.

In Personal Harmony Hall members and attendants of the Manchu
Chinese imperial court are gathered to witness the young emperor's
selection of an empress and appointment of imperial concubines.
The hall is swathed, from high ceiling to floor, in embroidered
yellow satin wall hangings, except far upstage where a rear entryway
is closed by red shutters.

The throne-area, stage-centre, is a three-foot-high platform
approached by five sets of steps, three front sets and one on each
side. The steps have red banisters with gilt decorations. The
platform furnishings include the throne-chair, deeply carved and
ornate with gilded dragons, and a narrow table covered with yellow
satin embroidered with dragon designs. Directly behind the throne-
chair stands a three-fold screen, its centre section showing nine
gilded dragons and each of its two side panels showing a painted
peacock, the tail feathers highly coloured. Pillars to the rear of the
platform flank another highly decorated portable screen. At each of
the two front corners of the platform stands a dragon-ornamented
candelabrum. Each candelabrum holds a very tall lighted candle.
The hall is majestic and impressive, but the décor suggests extrava-
gance rather than discriminating taste.

Before the curtain rises, the empress dowager, the emperor, and
all other persons of the Prologue, except the Senior Princess and the
girl candidates, have already taken their places. The empress
dowager occupies the throne. The emperor stands immediately at
her right. Further front on the platform, stage-left, stands Princess
Ch'un; correspondingly, stage-right, the eunuch Li Lien-ying.
Below the platform and left and right, to the rear of the banistered
steps at either side of the platform, stand senior eunuchs, boy
eunuchs, and ladies-in-waiting.

36

Formal Chinese court music begins with the rise of the curtain. The Senior Princess enters immediately, stage-left. She moves in step with the music. She carries, on a tray, a jade sceptre and two jewelled purses. She makes a deep bow at the foot of the centre steps and then moves backwards, still facing towards the dowager, to a point just below Princess Ch'un. Li Lien-ying, meanwhile, descends the stage-right steps, goes down on his right knee before the Senior Princess, accepts the tray, ascends the platform, presents the tray for the dowager's inspection, places it on the table, and returns to his station. Immediately the music ceases and the dowager speaks.

DOWAGER: Emperor! The girl candidates will now be summoned, and you are to choose among them. To her whom you choose as your empress you present the jade sceptre, and to those whom you choose as concubines you present the purses. And remember what I told you!

EMPEROR: The Imperial Parent will please make the decision.

DOWAGER: As to that, I am willing to indicate to whom you are to present the purses. But you shall decide to whom you will give the jade sceptre.

EMPEROR: Since your minister is still very young, he needs your assistance.

DOWAGER: Our ancestors decreed procedure for the selection of an empress. I cannot decide for you. But remember what I told you. To choose not the prettiest girl but a good and loyal girl will assure happiness.

EMPEROR: This your minister understands.

DOWAGER: [to LI LIEN-YING]: Now, Li, we bid them enter.

LI: Your servant hears. [He calls towards off-stage right.] Have the young women come up.

[At once two eunuchs enter, followed by the Yehonala girl, the two Tatala girls, and the two daughters of Te-hsing. The five candidates stand in a row, facing the throne.]

LI: Old Buddha permits the ordinary salutation.

[The five candidates quickly drop to their knees, bow their heads, and rise. The Yehonala girl and the Te-hsing sisters now stand in line, profile, somewhat to the left; the Tatala sisters step to the right, facing the other three.]

DOWAGER [with an admonishing smile and perceptibly indicating, by

37

the turn of her head, the Yehonala girl, addresses the emperor]: Here is a daughter of the Kuei family. You have known her since she was a small child, and you also know that she is my niece. Next to her stand the sisters from Te-hsing's family and, over there, the sisters from the Chang family. Now [*judiciously surveying them, but also sending an eye-signal to* LI LIEN-YING] all the candidates are present.

[LI *bows at once, one knee bent. He approaches the table, takes up the tray, descends the righthand steps, and, with head bent, kneels and raises the tray high. The emperor slowly descends the central steps, takes up the jade sceptre, and then turns directly to the younger Tatala girl (that is, the later* LADY CHÊN), *who is about to kneel.*]

DOWAGER [*sharply*]: Emperor!

[*Patently terrified,* THE EMPEROR *tenses his arms, thus partially withdrawing the sceptre, which he holds with both hands. The Tatala girl, raising her head, looks at him directly and fondly.*]

DOWAGER [*her voice now less shrill but no less stern*]: Emperor!

EMPEROR [*retreating towards the central steps*]: Yes, Parent of the Empire?

DOWAGER [*her eyes pointedly fixed on the Yehonala girl*]: I say no more. But remember what I told you. Choose a good, loyal girl.

EMPEROR: Yes, Parent of the Empire.

[*The Yehonala girl has already knelt even before the* EMPEROR *turns towards her. The* EMPEROR, *still at the foot of the central steps, raises his head, meets the* DOWAGER's *eyes, drops his eyes, turns and hands over the sceptre without glancing at the recipient. He stands, expressionless, his head averted. The* DOWAGER *exchanges a smile with the eunuch,* LI, *and then addresses the* SENIOR PRINCESS.]

DOWAGER: Give the purses to the Tatala girls.

SENIOR PRINCESS: I obey.

[*As the* SENIOR PRINCESS *takes the purses from the tray and presents them to the Tatala girls, who, their faces showing dismay and potential rebellion, kneel perfunctorily to receive them, the* EMPEROR *has turned his back on the appointed* EMPRESS *and is watching the presentation of the purses. He then hastily ascends the steps.*

Just as he sets foot on the throne-platform, the largest candle in the candelabrum at the left lurches and falls to the floor. From the

38

line of eunuchs one (recognized later as WANG SHANG) *leaps forward, seizes the candle, and refixes it in its socket.*]

DOWAGER [*reacting as to a bad omen*]: Who was responsible for this?

WANG SHANG [*kneeling*]: May I report to Old Buddha, the candles were lit by Nieh Pa-shih, assisted by a new eunuch.

DOWAGER: Nieh Pa-shih has served in the palace for years. How dare he be so stupid! But he is old. Simply drag him out and give him forty heavy lashes. But that new eunuch. Haul him off the palace grounds and see to it that he is whipped – to death.

EMPEROR: The Parent of the Empire will please excuse them.

DOWAGER: Excuse them! They will only be more careless next time. It is not your place to be asking favours for such trash. [*She now addresses* WANG SHANG] Have those two good-for-nothings dragged out at once!

[WANG SHANG, *on his knees, shows no sign of compliance.*]

LI [*peremptorily*]: Wang Shang!

[*His face set and closed,* WANG SHANG *rises and withdraws, upstage. The* DOWAGER *stands. All present kneel as she moves forward, descending the central steps. As she reaches the lowest step, everyone rises again. The Younger Tatala girl, darting forwards, now kneels directly at the* DOWAGER's *feet.*]

YOUNGER TATALA (LADY CHÊN): Your slave renders thanks for the honour.

DOWAGER [*brusquely*]: Such thanks are unnecessary. Get up!

YOUNGER TATALA (LADY CHÊN): May I dare to beg the Empress Dowager, as an extraordinary favour, to excuse the two eunuchs?

DOWAGER: Since as yet you have had no experience of life within the palace, you know nothing about my ancestral laws. On such a matter as this no one is allowed to ask favours. Get up!

[*The* EMPEROR *promptly descends the left-front steps and kneels beside* LADY CHÊN. *As the* EMPEROR *goes to his knees, everyone else kneels, the ensemble kneeling to the* EMPRESS DOWAGER.]

EMPEROR: I beseech the Parent of the Empire, grant the extraordinary favour.

DOWAGER [*withdrawing up the steps*]: What are you all kneeling for?

LI: It seems, Old Buddha, that this is a day of good omen for the emperor. And considering the old age of that no-account slave, might you not excuse them both for today and take no further notice until tomorrow?

39

DOWAGER [*to* LI LIEN-YING]: Very well then, since this is a day of good omen for the emperor, we will proceed as you suggest.

EMPEROR: The Parent of the Empire accepts our thanks?

DOWAGER: Get up! We are leaving! [*She is addressing* LI.]

LI: Your servant hears. [*He shouts towards offstage right*] Old Buddha will use the sedan chair!

[*Moving off right, the* DOWAGER *tosses an approving nod towards the new empress and then, observing glances pass between the* EMPEROR *and* LADY CHÊN, *frowns.*]

DOWAGER [*severely*]: Emperor!

EMPEROR: Yes, Parent of the Empire.

[*His head bent, the* EMPEROR *follows the* DOWAGER *off downstage right. All other members of the company stand as though seeing nothing. As the curtain begins to descend,* LADY CHÊN *buries her face in her hands. Her elder sister, who has been weeping, steps towards her. The two sisters embrace in mutual commiseration.*]

 ACT I

The Consort Humiliated

Time: early summer, 1894, late afternoon.
Place: main courtyard of the South Lake Mutual Pleasure Pavilion.

Near the left wall of the courtyard a bamboo clump rises above a pile of stones overgrown with ferns. A moon-gate within the wall on the right (upstage) carried on its upper beam the inscription 迎翠 (literally *welcome blue-green*, symbolically *pleasure*). Downstage right and near the wall a rock suggests, by its shape, a large bamboo stalk. It is flanked by several plantains. Above the rear wall, far upstage, branches of a bamboo grove and roofs of the Mutual Pleasure Pavilion are visible. An entryway through this rear wall, with low steps visible, provides immediate access to the pavilion itself. Downstage, right of centre, stands a marble-topped chess table. On either side stand drum-shaped porcelain stools ornamented in the traditional five colours (black, white, blue, red, and yellow).

As the curtain rises, Lady Chin (the older sister of the emperor's favourite, Lady Chên) is strolling in the courtyard and watching, with mingled amusement and concern, two palace girls, Ch'un-yen and Ch'un-shou, who are playing with a large box camera set on a tripod. At a gesture from Ch'un-yen, Lady Chin, holding a fan, takes up a rigid, facing-the-camera pose in front of the moon-gate. Ch'un-yen dives in under the black cloth of this late nineteenth-century box camera.

CH'UN-YEN [*her head emerging again from under the black cloth*]: Looking through a camera is certainly very odd, isn't it! Everything is upside down! Even Lady Chin's shadow.
CH'UN-SHOU: Now let me look.

CH'UN-YEN: Well, just let me look first, just once more.

CH'UN-SHOU: You've been looking and looking. Let me look now. [CH'UN-YEN *concedes.*] Everything really is upside down, really! But still I can tell that Lady Chin is folding her fan.

CHIN: But now you two had better stop playing around. You might ruin the machine. [*She now turns towards the rear entryway and calls.*] Come on, hurry up, little sister. If you're going to take my picture, why don't you come and do it?

CHÊN [*offstage rear, as within the pavilion*]: I'm coming. I'm changing my clothes.

CHIN: Well hurry up. It's hot out here. Why should I stand around all this time? If you don't come right now, I'm leaving.

[LADY CHÊN *enters. She is imitating, with deliberate exaggeration, a young man's hasty stride. She wears black trousers, a long, pale yellow overshirt, a short blue vest, and a black gauze skullcap topped with a red coral button and ornamented, at the forehead, with a huge pearl.*]

CHÊN [*also imitating a boy's voice and offhand manner*]: Here I am. Here I am. Come on now. Greet me properly.

CHIN [*startled, and reproving*]: What a way to behave! And dressing up like a boy again!

CHÊN: But just look. Now! Don't I look like him?

[*She emphasizes* him, *implying that she resembles the emperor.*]

CHIN: All right, you give a good imitation. But I hope you don't start thinking you are the emperor.

CHÊN: Come on now. Everybody! Kowtow!

CHIN: Shame on you!

CHÊN: Well, all right. Then let's pretend I'm Old Buddha. Now watch me. [*She points to* CH'UN-YEN.] You be Li Lien-ying. I am Old Buddha.

[*Assuming the heavy, slow tread of the dowager,* LADY CHÊN *advances as if addressing 'Li Lien-ying' and points abruptly at* LADY CHIN.]

CHÊN: This one here. Shameless slave-wench. Haul her out! Give her forty heavy lashes!

CHIN: You've lost your mind!

CHÊN: I have not! Oh well. Let's take the picture.

[*Abruptly resuming her own natural pace and voice, she walks over to the camera.* LADY CHIN *resumes her pose, as of the scene-opening, standing by the moon-gate.*]

CHÊN [*about to put her head under the camera cloth*]: Don't hold your neck so stiff. You look like some silly girl trying to impress a boy. The whole point in taking pictures is to have people looking natural.

[*As* LADY CHÊN *thrusts her head under the cloth,* CH'UN-YEN *and* CH'UN-SHOU *run up and peer into the lens.*]

CHÊN: Get away from there. [*She points towards* LADY CHIN.] Don't move. [*She shoves in the film plate and quickly drops the lens cover.*] There. Now we have your picture.

CHIN: And now I'm tired.

CHÊN: Well, let's go in and you can rest.

CHIN: And you'd better take off that outfit and put on your regular clothes. If the empress comes over, she'll have plenty of tales about you to take to Old Buddha.

CHÊN: Oh, let her talk. She doesn't scare me.

CHIN: But all the same, she is the empress.

CHÊN: Hmph! Empress! Just because she's Old Buddha's niece. She's a usurper, that kind of an empress. Nothing very impressive about that.

CHIN: Must you keep on talking right out like this?

CHÊN: Why not? Just what can the empress do about it? Do you think she can eat us alive?

CHIN: That's as may be, but I say you'd better change into your own clothes. Just suppose Old Buddha herself comes by and catches you like this. Then we'll see some fun!

CH'UN-SHOU [*kneeling before* LADY CHÊN]: May I report, we've heard that Old Buddha is coming out to view the lotus flowers. She may come through here. We can't be sure she won't.

CHÊN: Nonsense. It's too early for lotus flowers.

CH'UN-YEN [*approaching and kneeling beside her companion*]: Your slave would be glad to agree with you. But our eunuch reported a single blossom already opened over here on South Lake. Since this is a good omen, Old Buddha is coming over on purpose to see it.

CHIN: Are you sure?

CH'UN-YEN: Your slave never dares tell a lie.

[CH'UN-SHOU *and* CH'UN-YEN *now stand up again.*]

CHIN: We'd better find that eunuch and ask him for sure.

CHÊN: But you can't. I've already sent him out to the Tung-hua gate, to the camera shop.

43

CHIN: Speaking of that camera shop, this reminds me – [*She speaks to* CH'UN-YEN *and* CH'UN-SHOU.] You go inside.

CH'UN-YEN and CH'UN-SHOU [*as they withdraw through the rear doorway*]: Your servant obeys.

CHÊN: What's wrong now?

CHIN: Just last night, less than half an hour after the emperor had summoned you to the Ying-t'ai, Nieh Pa-shih came over to speak with me. He said someone had told Old Buddha that it was you who set up that camera shop outside the Tung-hua gate and put the eunuch in charge of it.

CHÊN: Oh-oh [*expressing concern and dismay*]. And what is Old Buddha saying about it?

CHIN: Old Buddha is not pleased. She says maybe it is all right to take pictures here inside the palace grounds, but that camera shop just outside the palace gates cannot be permitted – because if people in general find out who really owns the shop, there'll be trouble.

CHÊN [*after a moment's reflection*]: The only one who would go running to her to tell her about this is the empress. And still our empress has the impudence to ask me to see to it that the emperor finds a job for the son of her wet nurse.

CHIN: But what's the use of getting into a wrangle with her?

CHÊN: But then why doesn't she behave like an empress? Can't she be anything more than a spy working for Old Buddha? She picks up some slander or other to pass on to Old Buddha about the emperor every day. And now she's started carrying tales about us too.

CHIN: Enough. Enough of this. Don't talk any more of this nonsense. If anyone overhears you, the worse for us. Come on now, take another picture.

CHÊN: People outside think we have such a fine life in here, happy as the Immortals. Nobody knows we're worse off than the poorest little housewives. And everyday, what are we doing? Bending our necks, docilely taking orders from those who won't give up one little inch of power. Instead they hate us. They hate us! They are deliberately burying us alive! This is no life at all. It's just misery!

[*Rushing into* CHIN's *arms,* CHÊN *buries her head in her sister's shoulder and sobs violently.*]

CHIN: Now, now, don't cry anymore. What's the use?

CHÊN [*raising her head*]: Here we've been, inside the palace, for six whole years. They won't even let us go visit our own parents. Big sister, how can I help feeling miserable?

CHIN [*with a wry smile*]: Don't cry anymore. You're not a child. Come take another picture. [*Turning her own head,* CHIN *flicks away her own tears with her sleeve.*] You were gay and giddy enough to go in for all this dressing up like a boy-emperor. So now! Shall I take your picture?

CHÊN: Now my eyes are all swollen.

CHIN: That won't matter. [*She calls towards the pavilion.*] Ch'un-yen! Bring Lady Chên's dressing case! Hurry!

CH'UN-YEN [*from beyond the courtyard wall*]: Coming!

CHÊN [*with childlike petulance*]: Big sister, I don't want you to take my picture now.

[CH'UN-YEN *and* CH'UN-SHOU *enter, carrying, respectively, a dressing case and a mirror. They kneel before* LADY CHÊN.]

CHIN: No more of this. Stop acting like a child.

[LADY CHIN *busily powders* LADY CHÊN'*s face.* CHÊN *grudgingly removes the skullcap and smooths her hair before the mirror.*]

CHIN: See? See what happens when you cry like that?

CHÊN [*to* CH'UN-YEN *and* CH'UN-SHOU]: That's all.

[*The palace girls, carrying the case and mirror, make a slow and obviously reluctant exit.* LADY CHÊN *and* LADY CHIN *go over to the camera.*]

CHIN: But you know I don't know how to take pictures. You'll have to show me.

CHÊN: It's very simple. All we need to do is change the film-plate. [*She is putting in a new plate.*] There you are. Just wait till I'm ready, then take off the lens cover, and then put it back on, just the way I did. That's all there is to it.

[LADY CHIN *puts her head under the camera cloth.* LADY CHÊN *takes position exactly where* LADY CHIN *had been standing for the earlier picture, a few paces in front of the moon-gate. Just as* LADY CHIN'*s hand is groping to reach and remove the camera lens cover, the moon-gate opens wide enough to admit the* EMPRESS, *who slides in behind* LADY CHÊN. LADY CHIN, *who has seen this in the camera just as she removed the lens cover, at once abandons the camera and salutes, with bowed head, bent knee, and half-lifted hand, palm upwards.*]

CHIN: May your fortune be kind, Empress.

[*The* EMPRESS *makes acknowledgment with an abrupt nod.* LADY CHÊN, *clearly trapped and a little apprehensive, makes the ceremonial bow.*]

CHÊN: May your fortune be kind, Empress.

EMPRESS [*ignoring* LADY CHÊN]: You two certainly do find ways of amusing yourselves. Even taking pictures of each other! I've already told Old Buddha, and I'll be right here with her when she comes to see for herself. She says she is delighted and that, one of these days, she'll have you make a picture of her.

CHIN: Empress, wouldn't you like to come inside with us and sit down awhile?

EMPRESS: Not at all necessary. It's cool enough now. We can sit down out here.

[*The* EMPRESS *seats herself on one of the porcelain stools. The sisters remain standing.* CH'UN-YEN *and* CH'UN-SHOU *emerge from the pavilion gate. They carry trays of tea and fruit. Kneeling, they present them. The* EMPRESS *takes a cup of tea and a piece of fruit, sets them on the table, and then ignores them.* LADY CHIN *waves the girls away and again, reluctantly, they withdraw.*]

EMPRESS [*ostentatiously surveying* LADY CHÊN]: In that boy's outfit you are even more fetching.

CHÊN: I put it on just for fun, to make a picture. If it annoys you, your slave will withdraw and change into her more usual clothes.

EMPRESS: Not at all necessary. But tell me, has he come here recently?

CHÊN [*suavely*]: Empress, to whom do you refer?

EMPRESS [*irked, but bland*]: Has the emperor come here recently?

CHÊN: These last several days, because of the troubles with the Tung-hsüeh, those reactionaries, in Korea, the emperor has been conferring with his advisors. Perhaps he is still over at Inner Strength Hall.

EMPRESS: When I was with Old Buddha this morning, I heard her mention this Korean matter, but I don't understand much about such affairs.

CHIN: This affair is a worry to the emperor. It's been three days since he's been here.

EMPRESS [*ignoring* LADY CHIN *and continuing to address* LADY CHÊN]: Last night did he summon you to the Ying-t'ai?

46

CHÊN: Yes.

EMPRESS [*with a lightly insistent smile*]: Well? Then you've discussed that other matter with him?

CHÊN: Because of the Korean troubles, the emperor is preoccupied. He doesn't eat or even drink his tea. Consequently, your slave has not yet mentioned to His Majesty that other matter.

EMPRESS [*her tone is icy*]: Very well. If you have not mentioned it. . . . Of course mine is a very minor matter.

[LADY CHIN, *who has been standing somewhat apart during this colloquy, quietly advances a step or two so that she can momentarily catch* LADY CHÊN's *eye. By her expression* LADY CHIN *is warning* LADY CHÊN *even more firmly than her words suggest.*]

CHIN [*directly to* LADY CHÊN]: Next time you really should mention this matter to the emperor.

EMPRESS [*ignoring* LADY CHIN *and continuing to address* LADY CHÊN]: I must trouble you about something else also. I don't know whether you are willing to undertake it.

CHÊN: Whatever service your slave can render, you are welcome to command.

EMPRESS: This may need a few words of explanation. For the last several years my second maternal uncle has been finding it very difficult to meet his expenses. It's true he has an easy post in one of the government ministries, but there are many demands, including, of course, his social obligations. He really doesn't earn enough to support his family. Every year he goes more deeply into debt. As the saying goes: A great person has great difficulties; the little people have little difficulties.

CHÊN: The situation for your slave is not to be compared with that of even the little people.

EMPRESS: Recently my uncle asked Hsiao-te Chang to mention to me that at Foochow the post for a general of the armed forces is now vacant. My uncle would like me to ask the emperor to appoint him to this post. If you would beg the emperor, rather soon, to grant my uncle this appointment, I shall be grateful. Would you be willing?

CHÊN: If you, the empress, chose to say just a word to Old Buddha, wouldn't this be more effective?

EMPRESS: But in recent weeks I have already had to ask the Venerable Lady to grant two other appointments. I dare not open my mouth again right now on matters of this sort.

CHÊN: If you were to drop a word to Li, the chief eunuch, this would be equally effective. Except for the power of Old Buddha, his is second to none.

EMPRESS: Stop joking. Serious matters should be discussed seriously. Now, may I trouble you to put in a word with the emperor? I know you have a generous heart.

CHÊN: In your slave's opinion, her influence cannot compare with that of the others she has dared to mention.

EMPRESS [*with open sarcasm*]: Is there anyone who doesn't know that you're the only person the emperor pays any attention to?

CHÊN [*maintaining a polite smile*]: Whoever begs a favour of the emperor can persuade him. Kindly excuse your slave for being so forthright. But she always says to those present exactly what she would say in their absence.

EMPRESS [*now thoroughly angry*]: If you don't want to put in a word for me, that's that. Just because you think you have the protection of the emperor, you needn't suppose you'll get away with all this impudence.

CHIN [*promptly, to the* EMPRESS]: Please don't be upset. She's still too young to know how to handle words properly. Please don't hold it against her.

EMPRESS: So you want me to excuse her! I only expect her not to hate me and that she'll put in a good word for me with the emperor. That's the most I can hope for.

[*While the* EMPRESS *is speaking, the eunuch* HSIAO-TE CHANG *has come in through the moon-gate. He catches her eye before the others observe him.*]

EMPRESS: Hsiao-te Chang!

HSIAO-TE [*bowing*]: My lady. . . .

EMPRESS: Summon the sedan chair.

HSIAO-TE: Your slave hears. [*He shouts.*] The empress summons the sedan chair.

CHIN: Empress, won't you please delay just one moment? Let your slave beg her younger sister to make her apologies to you. If, because she has upset you, you should become ill, this would be most unfortunate.

EMPRESS [*rising, and ignoring both sisters*]: An apology! To me? How could I dare expect such an honour? (*She proceeds towards the moon-gate.*]

48

CHIN [*urgently*]: Little sister! Little sister!

(LADY CHÊN, *standing by the chess table, makes no move.* LADY CHIN *then hastily turns and bows as the* EMPRESS, *followed by* HSIAO-TE CHANG, *exits.* LADY CHIN, *now thoroughly impatient, returns to* LADY CHÊN.]

CHIN: Look here, you've let her go away angry.

CHÊN: What of that?

CHIN: Won't you just go out now, before they start off, and say a few words to calm her down and avoid more trouble?

CHÊN: I can't put on an act just to get along with people like her and, besides, why should I flatter her?

CHIN: I'm not saying you should flatter her. I'm saying that you haven't learned to control yourself and that you're just headstrong and stubborn. If she carries off too many more ugly reports to Old Buddha, there'll be more than trouble. There'll be catastrophe.

CHÊN: What are you so afraid of? Even with them all working together to make me miserable, the worst they can do is put me to death.

CHIN [*putting her hand over* LADY CHÊN'*s mouth*]: The more you talk, the worse you get. But you know the whole vast Ch'ing empire is controlled by the Yehonala, by the empress dowager and her relatives. There's no use trying to fight them.

CHÊN [*pushing aside* CHIN'*s hand but holding it gently*]: Do you still imagine that the Yehonala crowd will remain in power here forever? Do you think that the emperor is still a helpless child? There'll come a day when we will take over power here.

CHIN: As to that. . . . Well, perhaps you are right. There is that saying: Even the good should not accept insult. And I do admit, little sister, that you're brilliant – and clever. But cleverness should include keeping a clear head. Think before you speak!

CHÊN (*hanging her head, but then looking up*]: It's not that I haven't a clear head, but just that, even when I know what is involved, having her insult me just makes me explode. You know, big sister, that I do have a quick temper.

CHIN: If, as you say, you do recognize what is involved, then take my advice and go make your apologies to the empress. There's still time to forestall trouble.

CHÊN [*petulant again*]: I'll risk death rather than apologize.

CHIN: Just a moment ago you were claiming to have a clear head. Why are you now again acting like an addlepate?

CHÊN: I've just now been deliberately rude to her. How could I have enough face to apologize?

CHIN: There is also the saying: The truly great can bend and still keep a straight back. Will you, for this once, take my advice?

CHÊN [*pleading*]: You are a dear good big sister, but don't force me into this. Let me wait until tomorrow.

CHIN: Tomorrow may be too late.

CHÊN: Well then, how about if I wait a little and go over later this evening?

CHIN: This is no matter to be dawdling about. Once she tattles to Old Buddha, it's already too late.

CHÊN: Well . . .

CHIN [*firmly*]: Go! Now!

CHÊN [*tearfully, and pulling* CHIN's *arm so that it rests around* CHÊN's *waist*]: Dear big sister, please try to understand.

CHIN [*taking* CHÊN's *hand and speaking softly*]: Please listen to your big sister and just go apologize, now, and without any more fuss.

CHÊN [*brushing tears from her eyes*]: Well, will you also be a dear big sister and go with me?

CHIN [*seizing* CHÊN's *hand and pulling her towards the moon-gate*]: All right, I'll go with you, but let's go!

[*At this moment the old eunuch,* NIEH PA-SHIH, *comes through the gate.*]

NIEH [*bowing*]: May fortune be kind, Lady Chên. May fortune be kind, Lady Chin.

CHÊN: What's happened, Nieh Pa-shih?

NIEH: Permit me, my ladies. I come to tell you that Old Buddha is very angry with you.

[*The two sisters exchange glances.*]

CHÊN: What's she angry about?

NIEH: When Old Buddha came over here to view that lotus blossom, we noticed she was already upset about something. And because just these past several days there's been that rebellion in Korea, the Venerable Progenitor announced that this one lotus blossom is a bad omen.

CHÊN: But what has this to do with me?

NIEH: Now she has turned on you. When Old Buddha was tired and some of the slaves carried her over by the bubbling spring for a rest, the empress came up.

CHIN: What was the empress saying?

NIEH: I was posted outside. I couldn't hear much. But I could hear Old Buddha was in a temper and she kept shouting about 'Lady Chên!' and the empress kept on mumbling something or other and Old Buddha is getting more and more furious.

CHIN [to CHÊN]: Now you're really in for it, just as I said. The empress is not going to be easy to handle now.

[At this moment the head of LI LIEN-YING is visible through the opening in the moon-gate.]

CHÊN [to NIEH]: Anything more?

NIEH: Nothing more.

CHIN: Very well then. Go back at once wherever Old Buddha assigned you. If you let her find out you've been over here, you're in for a terrible whipping.

NIEH: No matter. You saved me once and I still owe you many, many thanks.

[As NIEH turns to leave, the EMPRESS DOWAGER, leaning on the arm of LI LIEN-YING and followed by the EMPRESS and several attendants (ladies-in-waiting, palace girls, eunuchs), advances slowly through the gate. Her face exhibits barely controlled fury. NIEH attempts to fade back behind the bamboo bush upstage left and he is, in fact, partly hidden by the insurging entourage, but the DOWAGER has already seen him.]

DOWAGER: Where are you off to? You! You think I don't see you, you scum of the earth? Nieh!

NIEH [advancing and kneeling]: Your slave deserves death.

DOWAGER: So! Your legs can carry you fast enough, the moment I turn my head. Perhaps they carried you here ahead of me – with some news?

NIEH: Your slave would not dare.

LI: Swallow your lies, scoundrel. Tell me, just how many heads do you think you've got?

NIEH: Your slave would not dare.

DOWAGER: Well, what brought you here?

NIEH [uneasily]: Your slave saw that these ladies were not accompanying Old Buddha. Old Buddha was alone, viewing the lotus. Your slave thought you would not enjoy the viewing, being alone. He came to ask the ladies to join you.

DOWAGER [with a frozen smile, and permitting LI to assist in settling *her on one of the porcelain stools*]: This is indeed wonderful, your showing such concern for me. [*The frozen smile turns off and her eyes flash.*] But you do have your wits about you. You tell a lie admirably. Why aren't you slapping your own mouth. [NIEH *slaps his mouth.*] So you're trying to trick me! You're a spy perhaps? The truth now. What are you trying to cover up? Let's have the truth this time.

NIEH: Your slave dares not play tricks.

LI: Well then, who ordered you to come here?

[LI *is fanning the* DOWAGER *with a short-handled, round, banana-leaf fan.*]

NIEH: The emperor.

DOWAGER: The emperor!

NIEH: The emperor commanded your slave to . . .

DOWAGER: What did he command?

NIEH: The palace domains are so vast, the emperor says the ladies might not be aware every time Old Buddha perhaps wishes to have them in attendance. He commanded your slave to be alert in reminding the ladies when Old Buddha may wish them to accompany her.

DOWAGER [*scornfully*]: A good and devoted emperor! [*Portentously*] Tell me, are you in the service of the emperor or are you serving me?

NIEH: Your slave serves Old Buddha.

DOWAGER: So, slippery tongue! In my service, but here you are prying into my private business, spying!

NIEH: Your slave is not a spy.

DOWAGER: You dare argue with me? [*She addresses* LI LIEN-YING.] Have him hauled out. Forty heavy lashes.

NIEH [*beating his head on the ground*]: Mercy, Old Buddha. Your slave is not a spy.

LI: Nonsense! Shut your mouth! [*He shouts towards the moon-gate.*] Come haul out this monkey here! Forty heavy lashes!

[*Two eunuchs enter and hustle* NIEH *along. Just as he is yanked through the gate,* NIEH *manages to call out towards* LADY CHÊN *and* LADY CHIN.]

NIEH: You ladies will try to help this slave?

[LADY CHÊN, *who has, throughout this episode, been conspicuously miserable and angry at once kneels before the* DOWAGER.]

CHÊN: I beg the grace of Old Buddha. Pardon this slave.

DOWAGER [*exchanging with* LI LIEN-YING *a malicious smile*]: If any-one else tried to beg such a favour, I certainly would not grant it. But look who is here, begging! Lady Chên! Should I dare disobey her? So! Let her see what she gets for her begging. Li, order the eunuchs to give Nieh eighty heavy lashes. Then have them haul him back in here so that he can thank Lady Chên. We'll then ship him off to the work-gangs on the Amur River.

LI: Aye! [*Calling beyond the gate*] Listen, you out there. Let him have eighty! Heavy lashes! Then shoo him in here again. To thank Lady Chên for her great kindness.

EUNUCHS [*outside*]: Aye!

[*The thud of the bamboo whip and the cries of* NIEH PA-SHIH *punctuate the following interchange.*]

DOWAGER [*with a mocking smile, to* LADY CHÊN]: I strike down anyone you beg me to pardon. No wonder all the eunuchs say you are, my lady, very tenderhearted and generous.

[LADY CHÊN *stands silent, her face without expression.*]

LI: Does the emperor affirm that Lady Chên is loyal and honest?

DOWAGER [*bitterly*]: To the emperor's mind this old woman no longer exists. He hates me, and he hates the empress. He would be happy if we were both dead. And this is your doing! [*She is addressing* LADY CHÊN, *who bends her head slightly, as though both agreeing and also avoiding further encounter.*] But Heaven is against you. Look at me! I'm alive and healthier than ever. In a few months now we'll celebrate my sixtieth birthday!

[*For a moment everyone stands motionless. The only sound is the thud of the bamboo, upstage beyond the wall, a low groan from* NIEH, *and the voice of the eunuch, counting.*]

EUNUCH [*offstage voice*]: Seventy-eight! Seventy-nine! Eighty! Done!

DOWAGER [*to* LADY CHÊN]: You hear? Now he is well whipped. Now your devoted slave will thank you.

[LADY CHÊN *continues staring into space, avoiding the* DOWAGER'*s eyes. Two eunuchs drag* NIEH *in through the moon-gate and fling him on his knees in front of the* DOWAGER.]

NIEH [*faintly*]: I beseech Old Buddha, let this old slave die.

[LADY CHÊN *buries her face in her hands.*]

DOWAGER [*with her malicious smile*]: You ought not to beg for death until you have first expressed your thanks to Lady Chên. Get over there!

[NIEH *turns his head towards* LADY CHÊN *but otherwise does not move.*]

DOWAGER: Get over there!

NIEH: Your slave cannot walk.

LI: If you can't walk, crawl!

[*On his hands and knees* NIEH *crawls towards* LADY CHÊN *who, her face still buried in her hands, is sobbing silently.*]

NIEH [*softly*]: Your slave gives thanks to his lady.

CHÊN: Nieh Pa-shih! It is all my fault.

NIEH: Your slave does not think you are to blame.

DOWAGER: Who wants to hear such nonsense! [*She addresses* LI.] Go slap his mouth!

[LI *slaps him. Blood oozes from* NIEH'S *mouth.*]

LI: So you've really made up your mind to die! Say thanks to Lady Chên and get this over with.

NIEH [*almost inaudibly*]: Thank you, my lady.

LI [*to eunuchs*]: Now get him out of here.

[*Exeunt eunuchs, dragging* NIEH, *who is already breathing his last. They throw him outside the gate but themselves return, standing just inside the gate once more. The* DOWAGER, *meanwhile, has risen to her feet and is pointing at the camera.*]

DOWAGER [*to* LI]: What's that three-leggèd thing over there?

LI: That? [*He goes to the camera, lifts the cloth, makes a play of careful investigation.*] I wonder what this can be? Ah, now I know! It is called a camera.

DOWAGER [*taking a step towards* LADY CHÊN]: For some time I have been hearing that you know how to take pictures. Really, you are no doubt the cleverest among my people here in the palace. You also have some literary ability. I understand that you have been composing poems. You are something of a painter too. And now you are even able to work this foreign devils' machine.

CHÊN [*remotely*]: It simply helps me pass the time when I am melancholy and depressed.

DOWAGER [*coolly*]: Melancholy and depressed? [*Now she attacks directly.*] Tell me, who opened that photographer's shop outside the Tung-hua gate?

CHIN: That was . . .

CHÊN [*interrupting* LADY CHIN's *attempt to divert the attack*]: I, your slave, opened it.

54

DOWAGER: And you even have the impudence to admit it! It isn't enough with all the mischief you've already been up to, here in the palace. Now you're out to make trouble for the emperor by opening a shop outside the palace and setting yourself up in business. [*She now addresses* LI LIEN-YING.] Have that foreign devils' machine taken outside and burned.

LI: Aye! [*He summons two boy eunuchs.*] Take it outside and burn it.

BOY EUNUCHS: Aye!

[*Exeunt, carrying camera and tripod.*]

DOWAGER: Send someone to seal up that shop outside the Tung-hua gate.

LI: Aye!

[LI *bows, appears to be about to transmit the order to one of the boy eunuchs, but then suddenly kneels before the* DOWAGER.]

LI: May I report to Old Buddha, the business at that photography shop is flourishing. Wouldn't it be a pity to shut it down?

DOWAGER [*thoughtfully*]: Well – , let me reward you. I am giving that shop to you. [*She sits down.*]

LI: Thank you, Old Buddha. [*He touches his forehead to the ground and then rises.*]

DOWAGER: You should also thank Lady Chên. Though I have generously given you the shop, it was she, after all, who established it.

LI: As Old Buddha commands. [*He bows towards* LADY CHÊN.] Thank you, my lady.

[CHÊN *ignores him.* LI, *stepping behind the* DOWAGER, *proceeds to fan her. At the same time, he blatantly sticks out his tongue at* LADY CHÊN, *and, addressing the* DOWAGER, *observes loudly –*]

LI: Quite an impossible creature!

DOWAGER: Since she even overlooks me, how could you expect her to look at you?

LI: Exactly, Old Buddha.

DOWAGER: She even carries herself like an emperor. Aren't those even the emperor's clothes she's wearing?

CHÊN: These clothes are not the emperor's. Your slave made them with her own hands.

DOWAGER: Your wardrobe is already more lavish than anyone else's around here. You have red dresses, green dresses, every day something new. And now you even have boy's clothes.

CHÊN: We have no household law against wearing such clothes.

DOWAGER [*rapping the table and standing up brusquely*]: What do you mean, household laws! My words are the household laws! [*She addresses* LI.] Take those clothes off of her. Rip them off and tear them up! [*The* DOWAGER *sits down again.*]

LI [*bowing*]: Aye! [*Then approaching* LADY CHÊN, *he bows to her.*] Wouldn't it be preferable for my lady to obey the order herself? [CHÊN *stands rigid.*] Well then [*he raises his hand as if about to remove her blue vest*], don't blame this slave if he removes these clothes with his own hands.

CHÊN: How dare you! [*She slaps him on the mouth.*]

LI: Ow! [*He retreats, rubbing his jaw.*]

CHIN [*appalled*]: Little sister!

DOWAGER [*rising and shouting*]: Kneel down, I tell you! Kneel! Kneel!

[*Seeing* LADY CHÊN *still stubborn,* LADY CHIN *places herself between her sister and the* DOWAGER.]

CHIN [*urgently*]: Little sister: Little sister! You'd better . . . you'd better. . . . Kneel down!

[*Reluctantly, under the pressure of* CHIN's *hand on her shoulder,* CHÊN *finally kneels.*]

DOWAGER [*now standing directly over* CHÊN *and glaring down at her*]: Impudence! Even those who might want to kick a dog keep an eye out for its master. But you! Daring to slap one of my own men!

LI [*spitting*]: This is too much! She's even jarred my teeth loose!

DOWAGER: Look what you've done to my poor man!

LI [*promptly kneeling and snivelling, like a spoiled child*]: Your poor slave suffers all this, all for you, Old Buddha. Never in all his life has he ever been treated like this. Let Old Buddha send him home. Your slave is not able to serve Old Buddha now. [*He knocks his forehead on the ground.*]

DOWAGER: Get up! I'll take care of this!

LI: Thank you, Old Buddha.

DOWAGER [*to* CHÊN]: To strike him is to strike me. [*The* DOWAGER's *voice now rises to a shriek.*] Are you defying me? Will you now slap your own mouth? [CHÊN, *though still kneeling, looks up at her calmly and steadily. The* DOWAGER *now screams towards* LI.] Come here!

LI [*rising and bowing*]: Old Buddha!

DOWAGER: Slap her face!

LI: Aye! [*As he approaches* CHÊN, *she gets to her feet and looks him full in the eyes.* LI *cringes, retreats, and again kneels before the* DOWAGER.] Old Buddha, I can no longer be of use to you.

DOWAGER: What are you afraid of?

LI [*still kneeling but, with a gesture, summoning the two eunuchs who had previously handled* NIEH]: Bring her over here! [*With tiger swiftness the two eunuchs pounce upon* CHÊN. *They twist her arms and block her knees. She struggles.*]

CHÊN: Let go! Let go of me!

LI [*rising and bowing*]: My Lady Chên, this is, you understand, an order from Old Buddha.

DOWAGER: Slap her mouth for me! Slap it hard!

LI [*bowing*]: Aye! [*Ostentatiously rolling up his sleeve,* LI *raises his arm and is about to lunge at* CHÊN *when the* EMPEROR *appears in the gateway.*]

EMPEROR: Stop this! [*At his voice the two eunuchs release* CHÊN, *and* LI's *slap fans empty air. Her arms thrown up over her face,* CHÊN *plunges past the* EMPEROR *and flees through the rear exit into the pavilion. The company stands terrorstruck, all except the* DOWAGER, *and* LI, *who scuttles to the* DOWAGER's *side.*]

EMPEROR: Scoundrel!

DOWAGER [*addressing both the* EMPEROR *and* LI]: Stand where you are!

EMPEROR [*his voice vibrating with fury*]: Scoundrel! Are you defying me?

DOWAGER: I gave him the order to strike her.

EMPEROR [*taken aback*]: What is going on here? [*Through the rear gate the palace girl,* CH'UN-YEN, *rushes in, panting and sobbing.*]

CH'UN-YEN: Lady Chên! Our poor Lady Chên! She ran right into the wall of her room. She's lying in there! She doesn't move! What shall we do?

EMPRESS: Well, what shall we do? I'll go see what's happening. [*She starts towards the pavilion.*]

EMPEROR: Stay here. No need for you. [*He starts towards the pavilion.*]

DOWAGER: Stop there, right where you are. [*He turns and faces her.*] Here you are looking straight at me and you haven't even bowed to me. Your mind's on nothing but coddling that little bitch. [*She snaps at* LADY CHIN.] Go look after that sister of yours. If she

57

dies, no doubt the people will be ready to talk and say I killed her.

CHIN: As you command. [*She bolts into the pavilion.*]

EMPEROR [*bitterly*]: If she's dead, perhaps that's just as well. Perhaps it would be better if we were both dead.

DOWAGER: What's this? Are you conniving with her against me?

EMPEROR: Your minister would not dare.

[*The* DOWAGER *stands up, strides about, flings her arms violently, shrieks.*]

DOWAGER: Every one of you is against me! You are all trying to drive me into my grave! [*She shakes her fist at the* EMPEROR.] So you think because now you're in charge of state affairs you can defy me! Just let me remind you! You and I [*her voice now steadies*] are figures behind the screen in a shadow play. [*Now her voice is very even.*] We must stay together behind the paper curtain. [*She now turns abruptly to* LI.] Come! We're going! [*She strides towards the moon-gate, the entourage turning to follow her.*]

LI [*bowing*]: Aye! [*He leaps forward and takes the* DOWAGER's *arm, meanwhile also shouting towards offstage right*] Bring up the sedan chair!

VOICES [*offstage*]: Aye! Aye! [*Sounds of flurried activity.*]

DOWAGER [*at the gate, to* LI]: No, we are going to stroll awhile.

[*Exeunt all, except the* EMPEROR. *The* EMPEROR *now takes a deep breath and starts to enter the gate to the pavilion. But at this moment* WANG SHANG *rushes in through the moon-gate and hurries after him.* WANG SHANG *bows.*]

EMPEROR: You're still waiting for me! I'd nearly forgotten about you.

[*The* EMPEROR *and* WANG SHANG *now move downstage right, approaching the chess table.*]

WANG SHANG: Over at Inner Strength Hall the princes and ministers are still waiting, waiting for your final decision.

EMPEROR: I came over here to sound out Old Buddha's opinion. I wasn't expecting to run into domestic troubles worse than what's going on in Korea.

WANG: That's as may be, but still it is the emperor who must decide whether we negotiate a peace or declare war.

EMPEROR [*slapping the chess table*]: Order them to open the attack!

WANG: But in Li Hung-chang's report to the throne, doesn't he point out that the Japanese navy is stronger than ours, and doesn't he advise the emperor to negotiate for peace?

EMPEROR: But what can we do? Half the funds allotted for ships and cannon Old Buddha makes off with, to build the Summer Palace, and the rest of the funds disappear into the pockets of Li Lien-ying. Serves us right if we take a defeat.

WANG: The emperor is understandably upset just now. He would be wise to reconsider carefully.

EMPEROR [*sharply*]: Suppose the Japanese come here and occupy the capital, wipe out the dynasty, kill us all. What of it? This is the worst that can happen – and it might be the best, for everyone. [*He pauses.*] Go back now. Tell the princes and ministers to draft the imperial decree. I'll come as soon as I can.

WANG: Aye!

[WANG *departs through the moon-gate. The* EMPEROR, *in overt despair, pounds his fist against his forehead. He enters the pavilion. It is growing dark.*]

[The curtain closes slowly.]

SECOND SCENE

The Boat Pact

Time: April 16, 1895, early evening.
Place: as in the first scene.

Darkness has fallen and lamplight from windows of the pavilion
glows above the rear wall right and through the rear gateway.
Moonlight, high right upstage, throws heavy shadows from deep
eaves and the wall. Downstage is as before except for the addition of
a stone bench and a further small table. As the curtain rises, the
courtyard is for a moment empty, pervaded only by moonlight and
the sound of a flute in the far distance.

Then Ch'un-yen comes down the pavilion steps visible through
the rear gateway. She is followed by Ch'un-shou. Ch'un-yen carries
a lamp with a green shade and, in her other hand, an incense burner.
Ch'un-shou carries two satin cushions, a yellow quilted and embroidered table cover, and several incense sticks. Ch'un-shou heaps
the cushions and the table cover on one of the porcelain stools.

CH'UN-YEN: Here, let me light the incense while you go for the lute –
the seven-stringed one.
CH'UN-SHOU: Very well.
[CH'UN-SHOU *scampers back up the pavilion steps.* CH'UN-YEN *is
spreading the tablecover and preparing to light the incense.*]
CH'UN-YEN [*calling*]: Be careful! Slowly now! Don't scratch that
precious old instrument or drop it.
[*With the lute, in an embroidered case,* CH'UN-SHOU *comes running
back out.*]
CH'UN-SHOU: My lady says not to light the incense quite yet. They
haven't quite finished their chess game in there.

CH'UN-YEN [*setting the incense sticks aside*]: Lady Chên is always so gloomy now.

CH'UN-SHOU: Ever since what happened last spring, she's never been very cheerful.

CH'UN-YEN: I suppose we can't blame her, what with Chief Li slapping her face right in front of everybody. She just can't stand such humiliation.

CH'UN-SHOU: You know very well if it weren't for the emperor and Lady Chin holding her back, she would have killed herself.

CH'UN-YEN: And our poor emperor having to see his dear one suffer and not being able to do a thing to help her. Now he can hardly even get a chance to come to see her.

CH'UN-SHOU: And when he does, having to creep in here like some poor little thief, he's so scared Old Buddha will find out. And yet everybody in the palace imagines he's so lucky, with all the girls he could want and calling for them whenever he pleases.

CH'UN-YEN: And lately he goes around with his face longer than ever, as if he is always worried.

CH'UN-SHOU: As for me, it's my guess that it's what's worrying him that's what Lady Chên is really so gloomy about too.

CH'UN-YEN: How do you mean?

CH'UN-SHOU: As if you didn't know that our Great Ch'ing empire is at war with Japan!

CH'UN-YEN: But we've been defeated. It's all over.

CH'UN-SHOU: Exactly. Prince Kung sent someone to arrange the peace terms.

CH'UN-YEN: But doesn't this mean the war's over?

CH'UN-SHOU: Hardly. They can't agree on the peace terms.

CH'UN-YEN: Oh?

CH'UN-SHOU [*lowering her voice*]: Almost two weeks ago, I think it was, the emperor and Lady Chên stayed awake all night just from worrying about this. I could hear them talking.

CH'UN-YEN: What were they saying?

CH'UN-SHOU: What I caught, as much as I could hear, was something like the Japanese will make us pay for this and pay for that and pay and pay – who knows how many thousands and millions we'll have to pay.

CH'UN-YEN: No wonder then that . . .

[WANG SHANG, *a gauze-covered lantern in his hand, slips in*

61

quickly through the moon-gate, which is in deep shadow.]

CH'UN-SHOU: Who's that?

WANG SHANG: Just me.

CH'UN-YEN: Chief Wang! Then the emperor is coming?

WANG: He's still over at the Yi-luan Hall, trying to see Old Buddha.

CH'UN-YEN: Hasn't he seen her yet?

WANG: Not yet. Chief Li Lien-ying and Old Buddha are playing cards. No one dares tell her that the emperor is waiting. All he can do is wait there, kneeling outside the door. You can't help pitying him, just kneeling there hour after hour.

CH'UN-SHOU: Why should he stay there on his knees, waiting for her? What difference would it make if he just goes away and tries again tomorrow?

WANG: We're in really serious trouble, and the emperor has to get instructions from Old Buddha. These last couple of days, news from abroad hasn't been good.

CH'UN-YEN: Is it true the peace terms have been settled?

WANG: No, not yet. But, besides that, something else has happened.

CH'UN-SHOU: What is it now?

WANG: You know it was Li Hung-chang that the court sent over to Japan to negotiate. It's not enough that he couldn't get satisfactory peace terms. Now someone has tried to assassinate him.

CH'UN-YEN: No! What do we do now?

WANG: By luck Li Hung-chang wasn't killed, just wounded. But even so, this adds to the emperor's troubles. He and Prince Kung and the chief ministers have been in conference nearly all day today. Now he's trying to get instructions from Old Buddha, and there are Prince Kung and the ministers still waiting. They can't come to any decision without an Imperial Decree from her.

CH'UN-SHOU: And you mean to say that Old Buddha and Chief Li are just sitting there playing cards?

WANG: Most likely. You know Old Buddha favours her own men over any emperors. Look what happened to Emperor T'ung-chih, who was her own son, her own flesh and blood. You'd think she would have favoured him, but no, she had no use for him. Those were the days when she doted on the eunuch An Te-hai. Then whatever An Te-hai told her, Old Buddha believed.

CH'UN-YEN: They say that when Emperor T'ung-chih died, Old Buddha didn't waste even a tear on him.

WANG: And that's the truth. And since she didn't love her own son, why should we expect her to love an emperor who is only her sister's son?

CH'UN-SHOU: They say, too, that when T'ung-chih's empress killed herself, it was Old Buddha who forced her to it.

WANG: For that matter, didn't Old Buddha bring about the death of Emperor T'ung-chih himself?

CH'UN-YEN: Old Buddha never did treat Emperor T'ung-chih decently, and now she's acting the same way towards our emperor. Why does she act like this?

WANG: Who can understand such things? She just likes to step on emperors and pamper some pet eunuch, that's all.

CH'UN-SHOU: It's really fantastic.

WANG: Thirty years ago everything was An Te-hai. Nowadays everything is Li Lien-ying. You know that when she sent her dear little An Te-hai south through Shantung to get some embroidered dragon robes, Ting, the governor of the province, had the spunk to have An executed – and what's more, got away with it. But nowadays, with Li Lien-ying, it's not so easy. Even six years ago, when Li went with Prince Ch'un to the coast to observe the navy manoeuvres, everybody was forced to salute that eunuch Li just as if he were Prince Ch'un himself. That little nobody Li! But who would dare to cross him? The whole empire, it seems, is entirely in the hands of Old Buddha and Li Lien-ying.

CH'UN-YEN: Why does Li dislike the emperor and Lady Chên? Why is he always making trouble for them with the empress dowager?

WANG: Why? I've no idea. It's not as though there were any need for it. After all, though in theory the emperor is in charge of state affairs, everyone knows he is emperor in name only and that Old Buddha still has her grip on all the real power. Old Buddha can still dethrone the emperor whenever she pleases. But that still couldn't make an emperor of Li Lien-ying.

CH'UN-SHOU: A eunuch an emperor! Then people like us might get to be imperial consorts!

WANG: You'd not do so badly either, as imperial consorts. But a eunuch as emperor, that's quite another matter. [*He takes out a pocket watch.*] That late already! The emperor's surely gotten in to see Old Buddha by now. I'd better get a move on. [*As he is about to go out through the gate, he turns once more to the girls.*]

Before long now, probably the emperor will be coming over here.

CH'UN-YEN and CH'UN-SHOU [*with surprise and obvious joy*]: Really!

WANG: I'm not absolutely sure, of course. See you later. [*Exit.*]

CH'UN-YEN and CH'UN-SHOU [*somewhat disappointed*]: See you later.

[*A murmur, the voices of* LADY CHÊN *and* LADY CHIN, *becomes faintly audible from inside the pavilion.*]

CH'UN-SHOU: Sounds as if they've at last finished that chess game. We'd better light the incense now.

[CH'UN-YEN *lights the incense.*]

CHÊN [*from beyond the upstage wall*]: Come on, big sister. Wouldn't you like to sit outside for awhile?

CHIN: No, I'm tired. I'd rather sleep.

[LADY CHÊN *emerges slowly, down the steps and through the pavilion gateway. Framed in the gateway, she stops to admire the moonlight sifting through the bamboos beyond the eaves of the pavilion. As she turns,* CH'UN-YEN *and* CH'UN-SHOU *bow gravely.* LADY CHÊN *approaches the table and picks up the lute. A gust of wind stirs the bamboos and the sound of the flute comes in more fully. The smoke from the incense sticks rises.*]

CHÊN: Who's that playing the flute?

CH'UN-YEN: A concubine of the former emperor, T'ung-chih.

CHÊN [*reflectively*]: No wonder, then, that flute has such a melancholy tone.

CH'UN-SHOU: May I report to my lady that Wang Shang was here just now.

CHÊN [*pleased, but pretending only mild interest*]: What did he have to say?

CH'UN-SHOU: That just possibly the emperor might come here tonight.

CHÊN: Where is the emperor now?

CH'UN-SHOU: The emperor has been waiting to have a conference with Old Buddha.

CHÊN: But it's so late. Is he still waiting?

CH'UN-SHOU: It seems an urgent decision is involved.

CHÊN: Oh . . . [*She sets the lute back on the table and stands with her head tilted, as though debating with herself.*] You need not wait on me now. Go rest awhile inside.

CH'UN-SHOU: As you say.

[CH'UN-YEN *and* CH'UN-SHOU *go out through the pavilion gate.*

CHÊN *now strolls about, gazing absentmindedly at the moonlit bamboos, sometimes stopping as in debate again with her own thoughts. She adjusts one of the incense sticks. Finally she sits down, tunes the lute, and begins to play the melody,* Autumn Geese, *accompanying the distant flute. Midway through the tune,* WANG SHANG *appears again, coming through the moon-gate.*]

WANG [*bowing*]: May I inform my lady that the emperor is on his way here.

CHÊN: Good!

[LADY CHÊN *rises and retreats towards the steps of the pavilion. The distant flute music ceases. From outside the righthand wall come sounds of footsteps, murmurs, the heaving and grunting of the sedan chair bearers. The* EMPEROR, *conspicuously distraught and annoyed, strides in through the moon-gate just as* WANG SHANG *turns to open it.* LADY CHÊN *advances and kneels.*]

CHÊN: May fortune be kind, Emperor.

EMPEROR [*seizing both her hands*]: Come, stand up. [*He turns to* WANG SHANG.] Go quickly and tell them to move the sedan chair close in under the wall and to blow out the candles.

WANG: Aye! [*He starts to leave.*]

EMPEROR: Hold on! You and the others stand guard. Watch the back of the grounds as well as the front. Keep your eyes open. No one is to come in.

WANG: Aye! [*Exit.*]

EMPEROR [*taking a deep breath*]: I'm so furious I could die!

CHÊN: What now, my Emperor?

EMPEROR [*blurting out his fury*]: Li Lien-ying! That filthy eunuch! Even insults me to my face, in front of Old Buddha. I'm sick to death of this emperor business.

[*He hurls his hat on the ground and lunges downstage, stopping by the rock and fern mound downstage left.* CHÊN *picks up his hat and follows him, speaking affectionately.*]

CHÊN: Why are you going on like this? There's no use in your letting yourself get so wrought up.

EMPEROR [*with a sigh*]: For the sake of the empire, for the sake of the dynasty, I made myself go over there to the Yi-luan Hall to ask instructions. Li was playing cards with Old Buddha and there was no way, in decency, for me to interrupt them. There I knelt, just outside the door. But from where he was sitting, Li could see me the whole time. And he kept up the pretence that he saw nothing. When they finished one game, he deliberately urged Old Buddha to play another round. He managed to keep me there on my knees for fully another half hour.

CHÊN [*motioning towards the stools by the table*]: Why don't you sit down?

EMPEROR [*sitting down but continuing to talk with the same agitation*]: Finally I couldn't wait any longer. To get him to notify Old Buddha I had to hold up a bribe of twenty silver taels.

CHÊN: No! You mean that even the emperor has to give a bribe before he can speak to Old Buddha?

EMPEROR: I haven't mentioned it before, but this has been the routine for some time now.

CHÊN: But after you bribed him, then did you get to see Old Buddha?

EMPEROR [*nodding*]: Yes, now I've seen her.

CHÊN: Well, what did she say?

EMPEROR: At first, nothing except to ask questions. What was my opinion? What was Prince Kung's opinion? What was the opinion of my tutor, Weng T'ung-ho? I'd told her we'd all been debating this business all day, had gone over the pros and cons, reached no decision. Old Buddha still would not make up her mind. Instead she just asked how badly Li Hung-chang was hurt.

CHÊN: Didn't I hear you saying, a couple of days ago, that Li was wounded by one of the assassin's bullets?

EMPEROR: That's right. And now it seems that Li Hung-chang's having been attacked has brought public opinion to our side – and so the Japanese are agreeing to a truce.

CHÊN: But won't they now back down on some of their terms too?

EMPEROR: They're agreeing to a truce, but they still insist on their terms.

CHÊN: You mean we have to accept all their terms?

EMPEROR: I was against accepting them. But the empress dowager ...

CHÊN: The empress dowager what?

EMPEROR: The empress dowager says in all seriousness: 'We are defeated. For the victors even to allow us to negotiate for peace is a concession. Why shouldn't we accept their terms?'

CHÊN: Does the empress dowager realize how severe the terms are?

EMPEROR: Just as I was starting to remind her of this, Li Lien-ying deliberately interrupted, plainly set on provoking Old Buddha against me. 'The emperor declared war in the first place,' he says, 'without even coming to Old Buddha for instructions. Now he's in trouble, the emperor comes to Old Buddha for help.' That's how this Li talks. And, 'Well, well,' says Li, 'if the emperor doesn't favour peace now, what shall we do? Perhaps Old Buddha and the emperor should themselves go to the front and fight until they lose their lives on the battlefield?' That filthy louse!

CHÊN: Do you have to talk like this?

EMPEROR: Old Buddha knows perfectly well that we were beaten because she took the Navy appropriation and used it to build herself a Summer Palace. But as usual, whatever she does, she blames it on somebody else. She'll never admit she's to blame for anything. And now, with all that talk from Li Lien-ying, the Venerable Progenitor gets into a tantrum and scolds me and starts screaming, 'All right! We'll go to the front! We'll fight, you and I!' But then she grabbed Li Lien-ying and threw him out.

CHÊN: She was just putting all this on so as to force you to accept the peace terms, wasn't she?

EMPEROR: I was desperate. I just stayed there on my knees and asked pardon. So then Old Buddha said: 'You set the sail in the first place. It's up to you to pull it in. It's not my affair. Whether you keep on fighting or settle for peace, it's no concern of mine.' And then she chased me out.

CHÊN: Well, what do we do now?

EMPEROR: It seems to me there's nothing we can do now except settle for peace. [*He pauses and looks down disconsolately.*] I've despatched a decree to Li Hung-chang authorizing him to use his own judgment in signing a peace treaty.

CHÊN [*almost in tears*]: But, Emperor, doesn't this mean a huge indemnity and loss of territory and much, much more?

EMPEROR [*rising, but holding* CHÊN'*s hands*]: No help for it. Unless we settle for peace, what is there to do?

CHÊN: According to the peace terms, we're made to pay two hundred million silver taels. Do we accept this demand?

EMPEROR: What's the use of saying more?

CHÊN: But where is all that much money to come from?

EMPEROR [*fiercely*]: Money! [*His face takes on a frigid smile.*] We'd have money if Old Buddha would oblige with some of what she calls her private income and Li Lien-ying surrendered what he takes in from bribes. Wouldn't these two sources alone be sufficient to pay the indemnity? Unfortunately, even when the Great Ch'ing empire suffers defeat, even when we have lost face, and no matter how much territory we have to relinquish, Old Buddha and her toadies refuse to worry, just so long as they can hobnob at the opera and spend lavishly on amusements out in the gardens. The empire won't last much longer, this I know.

CHÊN [*sadly*]: Emperor!

EMPEROR: I am remembering that the last emperor of the Ming dynasty told his daughters he could wish they'd never been born the children of an emperor. I could say the same.

CHÊN [*with a wry smile*]: Emperor, don't let your mind run like this. The situation now is as it is. There's nothing more worth saying about it. Why don't you let me call my sister to come out? The three of us can have some wine and for awhile forget our miseries.

EMPEROR: Well, all right.

CHÊN [*calling*]: Ch'un-yen!

CH'UN-YEN [*appearing at the pavilion gateway*]: Yes? [*She then promptly kneels, acknowledging the presence of the* EMPEROR.]

CHÊN: Tell Lady Chin the emperor is here, and ask her to come out for a drink with us.

CH'UN-YEN: May I report, Lady Chin has retired.

CHÊN: Go see if she is still awake.

EMPEROR: Don't disturb her. You and I can have our drink together.

CHÊN: Very well. [*Addressing* CH'UN-YEN.] And we'll burn that incense that Prince Li sent to us.

CH'UN-YEN: As you say.

[*Flute music is again audible.*]

EMPEROR [*to* CH'UN-YEN]: And bring me a large goblet.

CH'UN-YEN: As you say.

CHÊN: Take in the lute first.

CH'UN-YEN [*approaching and obeying*]: As you say. [*Exit.*]

EMPEROR: I'm sorry. You were playing, and I interrupted.

CHÊN: But after all, music is of no great concern to me. I only play a little when I'm lonely and depressed.

EMPEROR: I would not blame you. It's now been two whole days since we've been able to be together. But if we were just a husband and wife in an ordinary little family, at least we could be together every day. The moonlight is beautiful now. And the shadow of the bamboos. And that flute. So little time to enjoy what is beautiful. CH'UN-YEN *and* CH'UN-SHOU *enter, place wine, goblets, and incense sticks on the table, and exit promptly.*]

CHÊN: Your speaking of an ordinary little family reminds your slave of the boat families she saw once in Canton.

EMPEROR: What is a 'boat family?'

CHÊN: You know, those poor creatures who live on boats in the Pearl River. They have no land, no houses. They were born on the boats, and they die there. All their lives, day after day, they row in their boats, there on the river.

EMPEROR: Do they really live in a boat, always?

CHÊN: Husbands and wives, they live just on their boat, dry their clothes at the bow, cook their food in the stern. There's a small cabin in the middle where they sleep. It seemed to me they had no worries, that nothing could really bother them. They row east one day, west another, needing only a steering oar. To live like that is to be free.

EMPEROR: Do such people, free and happy, really exist?

CHÊN: Your slave has seen such people, many of them.

EMPEROR [*relaxing and improvising*]: Here we are on the river. The water is green. [*He circles with his hand.*] Here is our small boat and [*pointing*] clothes drying in the bow, the cookstove over there beyond, and [*putting his hand on the table*] here's that cabin in the middle. Just two people, you and I. When we want to go west, we can. When we want to go east –, we go east. No need to move our belongings from hall to hall. No need to ask anyone for instructions. Free! At liberty! [*He looks about, as if searching.*] All we need is that oar.

CHÊN: If the emperor really wants it, we can make that oar ourselves.

EMPEROR [*draining his goblet and then echoing* CHÊN]: We can make that oar ourselves. [CHÊN *looks at him earnestly. He seizes her hands. His face is jubilant.*] Well, for you and for our people I must make this oar.

CHÊN: You mean this?

EMPEROR: Yes, I mean it. [*He pauses, and then continues in a level voice.*] These past several years I've given much thought to what needs to be done. Unless the central government is thoroughly reorganized, our dynasty cannot last much longer. From above

I'm under constant pressure from Old Buddha because she is afraid of losing her enormous power. From below comes the pressure of all those incompetent ministers, every one of them scared of losing his job and so always flattering and agreeing with the dowager, scheming to prevent the least change, in order to hang on to their sinecures. That's the situation, and it gets worse every year.

CHÊN: Well, is there nothing that can be done about the central administration?

EMPEROR: Of course something can be done. But, confound it, there's no man I can really count on, ready to work and capable. These last two hundred and fifty years, since our ancestors captured this empire, you know what's been happening. Since every Manchu receives a court pension so generous that he never has to think about work, practically every Manchu by now is just a good-for-nothing. Even the court officers are no more than a pack of loafers and scoundrels, all of them stubborn, selfish, afraid of anything new. There's not one of them good for anything.

CHÊN: If Your Majesty can't find a man of real calibre from among our own people, can't you perhaps find the right sort of man from among the Han, from among the Chinese?

EMPEROR: From the – the Han? From among the Chinese? Well, they do have capable people. But the barrier. . . . Could we cross it?

CHÊN [*after several moments' silence*]: The country is falling apart, and the end of the dynasty is imminent. [*She stops and looks searchingly at the* EMPEROR.] If the country collapses, then both Man and Han, both Manchus and Chinese, will be equal – as slaves. Why, at this point, should we still insist on keeping ourselves apart from the Chinese?

EMPEROR [*earnestly*]: I myself have nothing against them. But a good many of our old Manchu officials actually say outright that, if they have to surrender the empire of our ancestors, they would rather give it over to one of the foreign powers than put it in the hands of the Chinese.

CHÊN: This is just wild talk. They've lost their heads.

EMPEROR [*agreeing, but also insisting*]: But when my father was alive, even he said that. [*He pauses and then begins to talk rapidly and intensely.*] But I don't care any longer what he said. We're going to go over the barrier. I'm going to have to call in some capable Chinese.

CHÊN [*equally intense, and with a radiant smile*]: My emperor!
[*She moves closer to him, and he again takes her hands.*]

EMPEROR: This is what I must do.

CHÊN: The emperor will no longer be afraid when the others object?

EMPEROR: So long as you are with me, why should I care about their objections?

CHÊN [*filling the wine goblet and raising it*]: Well then, will Your Majesty drink?

EMPEROR [*accepting the goblet and pouring another for* CHÊN]: You drink, also. [*They raise their goblets to eye level, smile a salute, and drink.*] In Japan since the Meiji reform, that country has grown every day stronger and richer. Now even the Western powers do not dare despise Japan. If we intend to rescue our country, we must have a reform too.

CHÊN [*eagerly*]: There are lots of rumours about the Chinese in the south actually counting on you to start this reform.

EMPEROR [*nodding*]: And my tutor, Weng T'ung-ho, has also been telling me that we must have this reform.

CHÊN: If, with reform, this country becomes strong and rich, then we won't need to be afraid of anyone.

EMPEROR [*after a brief pause, and then dropping his eyes*]: But I'm afraid Old Buddha won't allow any reform.

CHÊN: If the emperor is determined on this, it's time he stopped conceding to Old Buddha.

EMPEROR: But after all, she is the empress dowager.

CHÊN: But after all, Your Majesty is the ruler of this country.

EMPEROR [*abruptly raising his head*]: You mean . . .?

CHÊN [*kneeling*]: Your slave does not dare. . . .

EMPEROR [*reaching his hand to her*]: Come now, get up. [*He looks around.*] There's no one here. Whatever you want to say, say it.

CHÊN [*eyeing him closely as she speaks*]: If the Emperor hopes to accomplish anything, he must take the vast powers of the empress dowager into his own hands. [*She pauses. The* EMPEROR'*s face is non-committal.*] For an emperor this is legitimate. Who can prevent you?

EMPEROR: Princes and ministers, all depending for their survival on the empress dowager, will stir up the Venerable Progenitor to keep on fighting against me. And her henchmen also have real power and they're all die-hards. As to others, who might be ready to support me, they have no real power.

CHÊN: True enough. But if the Emperor does not lead the way and seize the power, how can your supporters move or follow you?

EMPEROR: You're right, beyond doubt. But the dowager is too strong. I don't think I can outface her.

CHÊN: When she first came to the palace, did she have this great power?

EMPEROR: Most certainly not.

CHÊN: Then may I ask Your Majesty how she acquired this power?

EMPEROR: When she came, her position was low enough. But politically she had ways of finding clever people to serve her and gradually her power increased.

CHÊN: As your slave sees it, political influence is secondary. What the dowager had to begin with was the will to seize power. Once she'd set her mind to it, those she wanted to rise with her worked for her. For her they schemed to take over key posts. For her they were willing to risk their lives. Doesn't Your Majesty recall hearing that, when Emperor Hsien-feng died, just thirty-four years ago, several of the princes were still very powerful? But the dowager already had Prince Kung and Jung-lu and a few others on her side. Through them she had the other princes put to death. Then she stationed herself behind the curtain, had all reports on state affairs presented to her, and gradually brought all authority into her own hands. It's been her own steady determination that's built her die-hard party. For the past forty years she's been, in fact, the emperor – and beyond challenge. [*She pauses again.*] My emperor must now take this power into his own hands.

EMPEROR [*gravely*]: I have the will. I am determined to take this power. [*He suddenly recovers his earlier mood.*] And when I have this power, then I can make the oar myself. [*Putting an arm around* LADY CHÊN, *he mimes the thrust of an oarsweep and, looking directly into her eyes, he speaks with mounting animation.*] And when I have this oar, then this boat of ours can go east or west, freely, and we shall be free, wholly free, too.

CHÊN: And our country will never be humiliated again.

EMPEROR: Wonderful! [*Now he proceeds to refill the goblets and again*

presents one to CHÊN.] My mind is made up. Drink to this!
CHÊN [*raising the goblet*]: Beginning now? Tonight?
EMPEROR [*firmly*]: Now! Tonight! This moment!
[*Just as they are about to tip their goblets*, WANG SHANG *enters*.]
WANG [*kneeling*]: May I report to the emperor, Old Buddha has
sent Hsiao-te Chang here, bearing verbal instructions.
CHÊN: What's this? Old Buddha? Sending Hsiao-te Chang here?
WANG: It is as you say.
EMPEROR: Very odd. Hsiao-te Chang is in the service of the empress.
If Old Buddha has instructions for me, why wouldn't she send
one of her own men?
WANG: Your slave does not know.
EMPEROR: Well, send him in.
WANG: Aye!
CHÊN: And why would he be coming here so late?
EMPEROR: Their spies are planted everywhere. However I move,
they find me.
[HSIAO-TE CHANG *enters and kneels*.]
HSIAO-TE: May fortune be kind, Emperor. May fortune be kind,
Lady Chên.
EMPEROR: What's all this about?
HSIAO-TE: Old Buddha commands your slave here to bid the
emperor come to her.
EMPEROR [*agitated*]: But what is this all about?
HSIAO-TE: Your slave does not know.
EMPEROR: Go back and tell Old Buddha I've already gone to bed.
HSIAO-TE [*with a sly smile*]: Making jokes, are you, at the expense of
my head? Even if your slave had two heads, he wouldn't dare
take a false report to Old Buddha.
EMPEROR: Well then, say just that it's too late and that I'll come see
Old Buddha tomorrow. Just that.
HSIAO-TE: Could your slave even dare repeat to Old Buddha such
words from the emperor? We know the rules. No matter what
time it is, and even if the emperor really were sound asleep, the
emperor still must go to Old Buddha when she has a mind to want
to see him.
EMPEROR [*irritably*]: Then you needn't say anything. Just go!
HSIAO-TE [*rising*]: The emperor actually will not come?
EMPEROR: I am not coming.

HSIAO-TE [*menacingly*]: If there is trouble, see that you do not blame this slave.

CHÊN [*to the* EMPEROR]: Since, during our talk, you have already made your big decision, it will probably do no harm if you go over there for a little while now.

EMPEROR [*to* HSIAO-TE]: What trouble do you anticipate?

HSIAO-TE: Since Lady Chên is here, your slave cannot say anything more.

CHÊN: Say what you have to say. I won't hold it against you.

HSIAO-TE: Well then, may your slave speak?

EMPEROR [*peremptorily*]: Say it, whatever it is. Say it.

HSIAO-TE: Old Buddha doesn't want the emperor to be here. Old Buddha wants the emperor to return to the empress's apartments.

EMPEROR [*with a frosty smile*]: Go back to Old Buddha and tell her I am not coming. That's final.

HSIAO-TE [*scornfully*]: As easy as that!

[*As* HSIAO-TE *turns to leave, the* EMPEROR *suddenly infuses himself with an unprecedented and aggressive dignity, stands tense and assertive as a lion about to attack.*]

EMPEROR [*roaring*]: Scoundrel! [*Startled,* HSIAO-TE *sinks to his knees.*] Slap your mouth!

HSIAO-TE [*whining*]: Your slave deserves death. [*He slaps his mouth.*]

EMPEROR [*steady and imposing*]: Go! Tell Old Buddha, tell your mistress, tell the whole empire [*his voice takes on a triumphant vigour*] that where I am is where I most love to be, that where I stay, I stay – and no one gives me orders!

HSIAO-TE: Aye.

EMPEROR: Get out!

HSIAO-TE [*starting to scamper off*]: Aye!

EMPEROR: Come here!

HSIAO-TE [*turning and kneeling once more*]: Aye!

EMPEROR: If Old Buddha asks what I am doing, tell her I am making an oar for a boat.

HSIAO-TE [*puzzled*]: Aye?

EMPEROR: Now get out!

HSIAO-TE [*scuttling off*]: Aye.

[*The* EMPEROR, *watching* HSIAO-TE, *bursts out laughing.* HSIAO-TE, *hearing the laughter, turns for a moment but then bolts out of the gate. The* EMPEROR, *still chuckling, and* LADY CHÊN, *smiling, pick up their wine goblets.*]

EMPEROR [*saluting with the goblet*]: Our oar!

CHÊN [*returning the salute*]: Our oar!

[Curtain, rapidly.]

❦ ACT II

Reform

Time: June 9, 1898, about 8 p.m.
Place: Lady Chên's apartment in the Luminous Benevolence Palace.

A wide window at the rear of the room is flanked by two round pillars. Above the window is a large clock, deducibly a state gift from some Western nation. A door in the lefthand wall leads to an adjacent corridor. The doorway is curtained. Near this door, and below a long, horizontal landscape painting, a semicircular desk holds a large, shallow porcelain bowl filled with quince and finger-citrons. An antique sword hangs on the righthand wall. Along this same wall and upstage, beyond an antique couch covered with embroidered cushions, a door, also curtained, leads to Lady Chên's sleeping quarters. A rectangular teakwood footstool, flanked by two spittoons, stands in front of the couch. A large, circular teakwood table and four teakwood chairs occupy the centre of the hall. Above the table hangs a large kerosene lamp.

As the curtain rises, Ch'un-yen, carrying a tea tray, enters from the right, followed by Ch'un-shou. From the tray Ch'un-shou takes two cups of tea and places them on the centre table. Lady Chin enters, through the lefthand door.

CH'UN-YEN: Please, my lady, some tea.

LADY CHIN [*approaching the table*]: Very well. But where is Lady Chên? Why did she disappear right after dinner?

CH'UN-YEN [*in a whisper*]: Lady Chên waits at the outer threshold for her emperor.

CHIN: That child is as if dead to everything except her one concern.

Ask her to come take a little tea. Waiting outside like that, she's likely to catch a miserable cold.

CH'UN-SHOU: Yes, indeed. [*Exit, left.*]

CHIN: Though the emperor went to the Summer Palace to see Old Buddha, he should be back by now.

CH'UN-YEN: Just awhile ago, a senior eunuch reported that the emperor would not return until after dinner.

CHIN [*looking at the clock*]: But he should long since have finished dinner.

CH'UN-YEN: That's why, as soon as she'd finished dinner herself, Lady Chên has been out there waiting.

CHIN: But why must she go out there herself? Couldn't she have you watch for the emperor's arrival?

CH'UN-YEN: Of course. But Lady Chên insists she herself must watch for him.

CHIN: Well, I suppose we can't blame her.

CH'UN-YEN [*probing, but trying to appear casual*]: Isn't the emperor seeing Old Buddha because he's discussing those plans for reform?

CHIN [*gently reproving*]: What do you know about such things? Don't be meddlesome.

[*From left rear come murmurs and footsteps of two women approaching.*]

CH'UN-YEN [*noticing the sounds*]: Ah, yes.

CHIN: That is Lady Chên coming up.

[*As* CH'UN-YEN *pushes aside the curtain in the doorway to the left,* CH'UN-SHOU *enters, but stands aside as they wait for* LADY CHÊN, *who comes in slowly, looking tired and worried.* LADY CHIN *at once goes to her and takes her hands.*]

CHIN: Little sister, my dear stupid child. And your hands are nearly frozen.

CHÊN [*with a wry smile*]: I'm not cold.

[CH'UN-YEN *and* CH'UN-SHOU *go out, left.*]

CHIN [*teasing*]: Still fibbing! The truth here is that a mad little wife has been frantically watching for her husband. Aren't you ashamed of yourself?

CHÊN: You're a fine one to be ragging me. You can't tell me that you have been thinking about anyone else but him all day long.

CHIN: All right, we'd better not talk about it. Come, have some hot tea now. If you get a cold, he'll be having a heart-ache.

77

CHÊN: If you don't stop teasing me, I'll just have to sew up your mouth.

CHIN [*now sipping her tea*]: I'm really not making fun of you. Ever since noon I've been so anxious I've actually been having heart palpitations, real ones.

CHÊN: If he doesn't come soon now, I think I may literally die of anxiety. But, big sister, didn't you yourself assure me that Old Buddha really has given the emperor permission to order the reforms?

CHIN: So they are saying, but what of that? It's my opinion that if the emperor decides on reform, he should proceed with reform. Why must he still go asking permission of Old Buddha.

CHÊN: But you know Old Buddha can't stand to have anyone start anything without informing her first. If the emperor does not ask her permission first and then tomorrow she hears about it, that would be disastrous. Listen!

[LADY CHÊN *hurries to the window and looks out.* LADY CHIN *stands, as if about to join her at the window.*]

CHIN: He's coming?

CHÊN [*disconsolate, and already returning to the table*]: No, I don't see anyone.

CHIN [*tenderly*]: Little sister, there's no use worrying yourself like this. Sit down and take your tea. Sooner or later he'll come.

CH'UN-YEN and CH'UN-SHOU [*calling in through the curtained doorway, left*]: He's coming!

CHÊN [*smiling towards* LADY CHIN]: He really is! I did hear him coming!

[*Shouts of sedan chair carriers float up from below stairs.* LADY CHÊN, *rushing again to the window, presses the palm of her hand to her breast.*]

CHÊN: What ails me? My heart is thudding so!

CHIN: Now he's coming, why are you so upset?

[*At the window* CHÊN *leans out. Footsteps sound clearly from below.* CHÊN *thrusts the window shut and turns towards* LADY CHIN.]

CHÊN: I can tell that he is upset. He's walking slowly. He looks tired. If Old Buddha . . . [*She presses her hand to her forehead.*]

CHIN [*taking* CHÊN's *hands*]: Don't say it. You'll start my heart thudding again too.

[*Sounds of footsteps on the stairs are followed by the quiet entrance*

78

of WANG SHANG, *carrying a documents box. He bows to* LADY CHÊN *and* LADY CHIN.]

WANG: May fortune be kind, my ladies.

[*Having placed the box on the round table,* WANG *returns to stand beside the door.* CH'UN-YEN *and* CH'UN-SHOU *hold the curtain high and aside. After a three-second pause, the* EMPEROR *finally appears,* LADY CHÊN *and* LADY CHIN *kneel, and* WANG SHANG, CH'UN-YEN, *and* CH'UN-SHOU *go out, dropping the curtain over the doorway.*]

EMPEROR [*stepping forwards at once, with a hand to each of the sisters*]: Stand up now. [*He smiles towards* CHÊN.] Our oar will soon be ready.

CHIN: What is this oar?

EMPEROR: Old Buddha has given permission for the reform, given it more readily than I could have dared expect.

CHÊN [*delighted, but with her hand again pressed hard against her breast*]: Permission? She has given you permission?

EMPEROR [*taking both her hands*]: Yes, truly. But your hands, why are they so cold?

CHIN: Because she's been standing outside for so long.

EMPEROR: But where?

CHÊN: I've not been anywhere.

CHIN: She's been waiting for the emperor, down there outside the door.

EMPEROR: Oh? I'm sorry. At first I was going to send someone to tell you the good news, but then I thought with such news I should tell you myself.

[CH'UN-YEN *enters with another tea-tray.*]

CHÊN: Emperor, please take some tea.

EMPEROR [*to* CH'UN-YEN]: Just set it over there.

CH'UN-YEN [*bowing*]: As you say.

[*She places the tray on the table and exits. The* EMPEROR *and the two sisters seat themselves at the table.*]

EMPEROR [*speaking rapidly and with pleased excitement*]: I went to see Old Buddha very early this morning – just after she had been having one of the eunuchs whipped, the one who combs her hair.

CHIN: What is she beating people up for now?

EMPEROR: Just some petty business or other.

CHIN: Probably because the old lady's hair is getting thin.

79

EMPEROR: Exactly. The empress dowager asked the eunuch, 'Is my hair falling out?' And the stupid eunuch had to be honest and say, the simpleton, 'Yes, your hair is falling out.' And she said, 'If my hair is falling out, make it grow in again!' Now how's the poor fellow to manage that?

CHIN: So what happened?

CHÊN: Big sister, please don't interrupt like this. Emperor, after you saw the empress dowager, what did she say?

EMPEROR: Since I could see she was in a fury, I didn't say anything for awhile. After lunch I went with her to see a play. Yang Hsiao-lou, the famous Yang, was performing, and gradually the Venerable Progenitor really became quite cheerful. Then, cautiously, I began to mention the matter of reform.

CHÊN: And what did she say?

EMPEROR: At first she just looked at me sharply, but she did listen. And as I explained further, she began to nod her head. She said, 'If you must make these reforms, I will not stop you. But do not infringe upon our ancestral rules. And don't give authority in these reforms to any Chinese.'

CHÊN: Is that all she said?

EMPEROR [*with an amused smile*]: She added, 'I've heard that you are studying English. Do you want to turn into a treacherous foreign devil?'

CHIN: They say that's what Li calls you behind your back – 'treacherous foreign devil'.

EMPEROR: That son of a turtle!

[CH'UN-YEN *enters*.]

CH'UN-YEN: May I report, the empress is sending Chief Eunuch Ting over here to invite you to come play chess.

CHÊN: Oh, I forgot about that. You tell him we're not coming.

CHIN: Let me go, anyhow. If none of us goes, she'll think we're deliberately ignoring her.

EMPEROR: Well, then. Yes, it will help if you will go.

CHIN: Yes, I think this is best. [*To* CH'UN-YEN] Order a sedan chair for me.

CH'UN-YEN: Yes indeed.

CHIN [*rising and bowing*]: Well, your slave departs.

CHÊN: Kindly give her my regards.

CHIN: Of course. [*Exit, left.*]

CHÊN [*turning at once to the* EMPEROR]: And now what else did the dowager say?

EMPEROR [*frowning*]: That's all – except that she told me to dismiss my tutor, Weng.

CHÊN [*startled*]: Dismiss Weng! And has the emperor agreed to this?

EMPEROR [*stammering*]: If – if I – if I didn't agree, the whole reform movement could be lost.

CHÊN [*wearily*]: I gather the emperor has agreed.

EMPEROR [*his head bowed*]: What else is there for me to do? [*He lifts his head again.*] But even so. . . . But even so, you don't have to be so unhappy. Just wait. When I have taken all the power into my own hands, finished making our oar – then it will be easy. I'll just invite Weng back again. [CHÊN *is obviously not reassured, she is not looking at him, and her head and shoulders are tense with fatigue and disappointment, but the* EMPEROR *is too preoccupied to notice.*] And, see here! I've drafted the reform decree. Let me show it to you. [*He opens the message box, takes out several closely written pages, and places them in front of her. She studies the opening lines.*]

CHÊN: I see you've been working it out very carefully.

EMPEROR [*running his finger down each line as he reads*]: You notice how I've handled it? 'We consider that, so long as national policy is not clearly defined, state commands are not likely to be fully obeyed. Among competing factions uncertainties aggravate differences incompatible as water and fire. These factions, recapitulating all the old errors of the Sung and Ming dynasties, exhaust themselves in arguments instead of attending to state affairs. Let us, therefore, remind ourselves of the fundamental principles and laws of China. Of old, the five emperors and three kings did not maintain identical policies. As need required, they replaced winter furs with summer homespuns, not expecting the use of both in the same season.' Reading sentences like these, can the conservative old officials have any objections? Isn't the reform to meet the changing needs of our time?

CHÊN [*following further lines with her finger and reading out in full voice*]: And these sentences express their meaning very well: 'But still we need an enlightened public opinion. We still need a wider common understanding about the need for change and reform. Self-interested officials, insisting on old ways and rejecting all new ideas, still engage in endless and futile debate.'

EMPEROR and LADY CHÊN [*reading aloud together*]: 'Let us recognize that, in our present situation, our power as a nation has perilously declined. With our undisciplined soldiers and inequably assigned funds, our scholars lacking knowledge of practical affairs, our workers lacking efficient direction, our weakness against the foreigners' aggressive strength, our poverty against their wealth, how can we expect to hold out against their trained troops and powerful weapons?' [*They exchange approving smiles.*]

CHÊN: Well written! Points well made!

EMPEROR: When I wrote it, it came all at once, all in one breath.

CHÊN: As a decree to announce the reform, it is work well done. But for the reform itself, the major work, we still must find men capable of carrying it through.

EMPEROR: Good old Weng, my tutor, has already made a recommendation. The man he speaks of has, says Weng, knowledge and ability ten times greater than his own.

CHÊN: And this man is?

EMPEROR: He is K'ang Yu-wei. I have summoned him to meet with me in the Hall of Efficient Administration early on the morning of the 16th.

CHÊN: And how is your good old tutor Weng?

EMPEROR: Ten days ago he asked for a week's vacation and he's still away. Somehow I must manage to retain him in his tutor's appointment.

CHÊN: It's common talk that the conservatives forced him to ask for that vacation, part of their plan towards getting him permanently expelled from the court.

EMPEROR [*indicating that he is already aware of this*]: He knows, of course, that in a few days I shall be proclaiming the reform. Foreseeing that Old Buddha would very likely take some action against him, he asked for permission to go away.

CHÊN: We know Old Buddha is set on dismissing him. But doesn't the emperor intend to protect him?

EMPEROR: Of course I intend to protect him, but . . .

CHÊN: Our Weng is not only your tutor but one major official you can absolutely rely on to support your plans. Even beyond the fact that he is the emperor's tutor he is already famous and deeply respected. If you let him be dismissed, this will dishearten all the others who are now in favour of reform.

EMPEROR: Letting him be dismissed may be good strategy, may help delay attack by our opponents.

CHÊN: But, Emperor, especially now right at the beginning of the reform, you must not yield even one point to the dowager. To give in at all, at once weakens your power.

EMPEROR: Just let me consider.

CHÊN: Right now – of all times, right now, and on this matter, the emperor must make up his mind at once. Certainly Old Buddha, as you must be aware, never dismissed those who were close to her and whom she trusted.

EMPEROR: But in the old days didn't she dismiss Prince Kung and Jung-lu?

CHÊN: Only after she already had all the power in her own hands. She never dismissed her close personal followers. [*She pauses. The* EMPEROR *appears attentive, as if in agreement.*] And what's more, four years ago, why did she restore Prince Kung and Jung-lu? Simply because it now served her interests to do so. Old Buddha always puts her own interests first.

EMPEROR: Very well. Tomorrow I'll talk to the dowager again.

CHÊN: And you really will talk to her about Weng?

EMPEROR: Certainly I will talk to her. . . . [*He calls towards offstage left.*] Wang, come here!

WANG [*answering offstage*]: Aye! [*Enters.*]

EMPEROR [*indicating the documents box*]: Take it and have them proclaim it.

WANG [*taking up the box*]: Aye!

EMPEROR [*still addressing* WANG]: As soon as court is over tomorrow morning, have a sedan chair ready. I'll be going out to the summer palace to see the empress dowager.

WANG: Aye! [*Exit.*]

[LADY CHÊN *turns to the* EMPEROR *with an approving smile, which he answers with a smile, though a somewhat tentative one. Holding hands, the two approach stage centre. Lights dim rapidly to full dark.*]

At the Lake

Time: September 15, 1898, evening of the Buddha's birthday, the Buddha who saves souls.
Place: by the lake on the Summer Palace grounds several miles outside Peking.

A dark-blue star-filled sky, without a moon, discloses at first only the farther shore of the lake and the distant Longevity Hill, on which the rooflines of the High-Ranging-Clouds Pavilion are dimly visible. Slowly expanding starlight gradually discloses a broad marble railing above the near shore of the lake. This railing zigzags from left to right. To the right there is a long stone bench. From boats far away over the lake there comes the sound of a drum and occasional music on strings. Except for the distant skyline and the upstage centre area with the railing and the stone bench, the stage remains dark. The emperor and Lady Chên, visible only as shadowy figures, are leaning, half-face towards the lake, against the marble railing.

EMPEROR: See, out on the lake now the lights are being set out on the marble boat.
CHÊN [*in a tone both despairing and scornful*]: Our stone boat! Our navy!
EMPEROR [*dryly*]: Yes, there's our navy – that marble, immovable boat, a boat going nowhere, a decorative piece for a festival! [*As he concludes, he slaps at the railing.*]
CHÊN: But why get wrought up about it now? After all, the Summer Palace and the marble boat have already been here more than three years. Why disturb yourself about it now?

EMPEROR: You'd rather I weren't disturbed? How can I help being disturbed? Here I've issued the decree for reform and worn myself out over it, and it's been insults and more insults now for one hundred days. I thought we could develop plans gradually, could slowly reorganize the central administration. But already everything goes from bad to worse, and my every least move towards reform produces only more trouble and more resistance. How do you expect me to control myself? Why shouldn't I be, as you say, wrought up?

[*He turns and seats himself on the stone bench.* LADY CHÊN, *after a moment's pause, seats herself beside him. The music, especially the drumbeat, becomes increasingly audible.*]

CHÊN: You must at least try to be patient, Your Majesty. A reform can't be accomplished in just a few months. Even tonight's festival must have required eight or ten days in preparation.

EMPEROR: But if only I had paid attention to your advice and . . .

CHÊN: That's no point now. We can try again. Why go on lamenting?

EMPEROR [*berating himself*]: Because back when the dowager dismissed our good old tutor, Weng, I did not listen to you, I did not speak up firmly enough. So now, among all the major Manchu officials, now only Li Tuan-fen and Chang Yin-huan still support me. All the rest are now the dowager's men. To my face they pretend to obey me, but they take their orders actually from the dowager and work only to make trouble for me.

CHÊN: As your slave sees it, the reformers and the conservatives will never be reconciled now. We've nothing to expect now but storm winds and high waves.

EMPEROR: That is what K'ang Yu-wei says. And now that Jung-lu has asked me to accompany the empress dowager for that inspection of troops at Tientsin, K'ang Yu-wei says it's part of a plot contrived by the dowager and those around her.

CHÊN: Exactly. It's the old trick, luring the tiger out of his mountains. While you're in Tientsin inspecting troops, all the reformers in Peking will be arrested and, by the time you return, it will be too late to save them.

EMPEROR: That's what they're scheming, of course. And so I do not want to go. But there's still the fact that Old Buddha has promised Jung-lu that she and I will inspect troops on October 20th in Tientsin.

CHÊN: But it would be much wiser for Your Majesty not to go.

EMPEROR [*his head bent*]: But Old Buddha insists that I go look at this new army Jung-lu has trained. How can I simply refuse to go? Even if I did refuse, wouldn't they then just contrive some other trap?

CHÊN [*counting on her fingers*]: Until October 20th you still have more than a month, a month and five days. In that time can't Your Majesty manage to deal with the situation?

EMPEROR [*indignantly*]: I've already been challenging the dowager all these months, but she still holds all the real political power. What more can I do?

CHÊN: Well then, why doesn't Your Majesty proceed at once to take over control of the military? It might be as well to appear calm and avoid any more direct struggle with the conservatives until you have actual command of the armed forces. Then, without any further risk of obstruction from the empress dowager, you can proceed to implement your reforms.

EMPEROR [*enthusiastically, and seizing* CHÊN's *hands*]: This is exactly what I've been thinking about. Tomorrow I'm planning to summon Yüan Shih-k'ai with just this in mind. [*He speaks now even more emphatically, and with gestures.*] I know he's a good general, and he's already proven his skill in Korea, and he suppressed the civil war there. He has courage. I'm planning to appoint him to train the new army. What do you think of the idea?

CHÊN: Your slave understands that Yüan Shih-k'ai is very capable but wonders whether or not he is dependable.

EMPEROR [*with a confident smile*]: Until now he has been assigned outside Peking. Further, he is not one of the dowager's henchmen. Why are you so suspicious of him?

[*Music from the lake increases, together with a hum of voices. Small lights appear at the far edge of the lake. The* EMPEROR *and* LADY CHÊN *rise and stand again by the railing. Footsteps sound off-stage right.*]

CHÊN: All the flares are ready over there now. Very soon Old Buddha will arrive to view the lighting of the lotus candles. We'd better be prepared to welcome her.

EMPEROR [*turning his head, listening*]: Old Buddha's already coming. Quick!

[*The rhythmic footsteps of sedan chair carriers and the accompany-*

ing attendants penetrate the dark, downstage right – with an occasional shout, as from the carriers, also.]
CHÊN: Why the hurry? The chair will pass on the main road, and we will greet her. It won't come here.
EMPEROR: All the same, a chair has stopped!
[*They both peer through the darkness towards the right.*]
CHÊN: Someone's coming!
[*Offstage shouts increase. The* EMPEROR *leaps up onto the marble railing, helps* LADY CHÊN *up beside him, and they run swiftly and softly along the rail down towards the left, dropping from the rail into the darkness.*]
EMPEROR [*as they are about to disappear over the rail (downstage left)*]: Quickly now. We'll go meet her chair.
[*Just as the two disappear, a young eunuch,* TS'UI YÜ-KUEI, *appears out of the darkness at the left, coming along inside the rail which the* EMPEROR *and* LADY CHÊN *have just crossed. He appears timid and calls very softly.*]
TS'UI YÜ-KUEI: Who's that here?
[TS'UI *looks about cautiously as he crosses over, downstage, as though he is seeing, or expects to see, ghosts. Music from the lake comes in more fully, but through it* TS'UI'*s voice comes, now with a firm tone. He reports in the darkness at the right.*]
TS'UI: May I report to Old Buddha, there is no one here.
DOWAGER: Nonsense! I saw them clearly. Two people!
TS'UI [*a little farther offstage*]: Aye!
[*Light increases slightly. The* EMPRESS DOWAGER *and* LI LIEN-YING *emerge from the shadows, followed by several eunuchs.*]
DOWAGER [*to* LI, *and indicating the other eunuchs*]: Tell them to stay outside. We don't want them in here.
LI: All right, you! Outside! Don't come in here. [*Exeunt eunuchs.*]
DOWAGER [*moving directly to the railing, near the stone bench*]: Here we'll have a good view of them lighting the candles on the lotus pads. We'll rest here awhile.
LI [*standing beside her and looking off across the lake*]: Aye! A good place they found, to talk over matters close to their hearts.
DOWAGER: They?
LI: Now who could 'they' be, Old Buddha? None other than the emperor and Lady Chên.
DOWAGER [*slyly*]: Oh, were they here a moment ago? Ask them to

return. I'll find out if, behind my back, they've been planning something against me.

LI [*with equal slyness*]: Why should Old Buddha trouble herself? Let them do as they please. No matter how clever they are, they can never be beyond your reach.

DOWAGER [*complacently*]: Even so, I'll enjoy finding out what plans they're making now.

LI: Your slave has been observing him and concludes that the emperor can think of no plans beyond listening to the advice of K'ang Yu-wei and all his little monkey tribe. Since K'ang Yu-wei has told him he need no longer show you filial respect, you can be sure he will follow this advice.

DOWAGER [*cynically*]: Tomorrow I will have this little K'ang fellow killed. We can then discover what other plans the emperor may have in mind.

LI: But if we wait until the emperor goes to inspect the troops at Tientsin, we can kill the whole litter of rebellious monkeys at once. This will be more exciting and more thorough.

DOWAGER: Be careful now. Don't let this leak out. Lately I have the feeling the emperor is deliberately saying nothing. Warn everyone to be especially cautious and on the alert. If you hear anything, tell me at once.

LI: Certainly. [*He gestures as if suddenly struck by a recollection.*] Ah, your slave did nearly forget. He must tell you he has heard that tomorrow the emperor is summoning Yüan Shih-k'ai and Lin Hsü to confer with him.

DOWAGER [*raising her head and rolling her eyes as if searching her memory*]: Yüan Shih-k'ai?

LI: The former imperial commissioner to Korea.

DOWAGER [*thoughtfully*]: I know. He's the man that Li Hung-chang's been promoting. I remember him – short man, round face, very gallant way with him. [*She speaks with decision.*] Tomorrow, after his interview with the emperor, you will tell him to come here to see me.

LI: Aye! [TS'UI *enters, again from the right.*] What now?

TS'UI: The emperor and Lady Chên are coming here to greet Old Buddha.

DOWAGER [*flashing a malicious smile which* LI *catches and shares*]: Well now, tell them I invite them to come up.

TS'UI: Aye! [*Exit.*]

LI: They really take us for simpletons.

DOWAGER: There'll come the day when I'll arrange death for them both.

[*The* EMPEROR *and* LADY CHÊN *appear right, kneel, and speak simultaneously.*]

EMPEROR: Your minister comes here to greet you.

CHÊN: Your maid-slave comes here to greet you.

DOWAGER: Stop all that! [*They rise.*] Where are you coming from?

EMPEROR: Your minister comes from the Lotus Fragrance Pavilion.

CHÊN: Your maid-servant comes from the Azure Cloud Cottage.

DOWAGER [*abruptly*]: And very likely you met each other by chance on the way. A coincidence, yes? [*She now speaks very slowly.*] While you were both on your way here, did you meet any other couples?

EMPEROR [*tensely*]: No. Even if there were, such couples would have fled away as soon as they saw your minister approaching.

DOWAGER: But I saw them, a boy and a girl leaning here against this railing. They saw me coming and they fled. Li, did you see them?

LI: Your slave saw them very clearly. But he reports to Old Buddha that they have taken a fine walk, made a considerable detour, and have now returned.

DOWAGER [*playing*]: To think they've come back again! [*She now shouts.*] Do you two think I'm just a blind old woman?

[*The* EMPEROR *and* LADY CHÊN *kneel, again speak simultaneously, and remain kneeling.*]

EMPEROR: Your minister does not dare to think so. Your minister deserves death.

CHÊN: Your maid-slave does not dare to think so. Your maid-slave deserves death.

DOWAGER: Then, after all, I can depend on my excellent eyesight?

EMPEROR: Originally your minister planned to welcome you from that side. Then later . . .

DOWAGER [*interrupting*]: Whether you were purposely trying to avoid me or not is of no consequence. But lying to me – this is a more serious matter.

EMPEROR: Your minister dares not lie.

DOWAGER: Hmm! Day by day you show me less and less respect. Who told you to neglect your filial duties?

EMPEROR: Could your minister dare to neglect his filial duty to the Imperial Parent?

DOWAGER: You do not dare neglect your filial duty?

EMPEROR: I dare not, Imperial Parent.

DOWAGER: Well then, will you pay attention to what I have to say?

EMPEROR: How dare your minister not pay attention to what you have to say?

DOWAGER: Well then, both of you, get up.

[*The* EMPEROR *and* LADY CHÊN *rise at once and, stepping forward, stand with their backs towards the lake and facing the* DOWAGER.]

EMPEROR: Thank you, Imperial Parent.

CHÊN: Thank you, Empress Dowager.

DOWAGER: Now that you agree to pay attention to what I have to say, I shall test you to see whether or not you will respect my commands.

EMPEROR: Your minister will assuredly obey you.

DOWAGER: Good! There is one person I want you to dismiss and punish.

EMPEROR [*agitated, but trying to hide his feelings*]: But your minister does not know who this is whom the imperial parent wishes to have dismissed and punished.

DOWAGER: He who taught you to disregard your filial obligations to me. K'ang . . . Yu-wei!

EMPEROR [*losing all composure*]: But . . .!

DOWAGER [*steadily*]: You have agreed to pay attention to what I have to say.

EMPEROR: That is so.

DOWAGER: Well then, you cannot say *no*, but must do as I say.

EMPEROR [*cowed*]: That is so.

[*Obviously determined on countering the emperor's concessions to the dowager,* LADY CHÊN *takes a step forward and is about to kneel when the* DOWAGER *addresses her.*]

DOWAGER: Chên, Miss Bright-and-early, don't bother to kneel. You want another favour, don't you? Can you have forgotten about Nieh Pa-shih who's still off there with the labour gangs on the Amur river?

CHÊN: But . . .

[*She is interrupted by a look and a gesture of protest from the* EMPEROR. *At this same moment the music from the lake becomes more insistent,* LI *steps up to the railing, and then turns towards the* DOWAGER.]

LI: Report to Old Buddha, the lamp-boats are waiting, waiting for you to observe the lighting of the lotus candles.

DOWAGER: Order my chair!

LI [*shouting towards offstage right*]: Old Buddha is going to ride! Step lively!

DOWAGER [*nodding towards the left*]: Hold on! Have them bring the chair around in there. We can try that detour too.

VOICE [*offstage*]: Aye!

DOWAGER [*to* EMPEROR]: After seeing the lotus lights, you are to issue a private order to the chief of the capital police to arrest K'ang Yu-wei, and from that point I will take personal charge of his case.

EMPEROR: As you say. [*He exchanges a glance with* LADY CHÊN.]

DOWAGER: No tricks now! You two follow me!

EMPEROR and LADY CHÊN: As you say.

[LI LIEN-YING *gives his arm to the* DOWAGER, *and they step along briskly. The* EMPEROR *and* LADY CHÊN *start to follow.* LADY CHÊN, *however, slips a bracelet from her arm, slides it into her small purse, pauses, exclaims, and runs back as if searching the ground below the railing.*]

CHÊN: But wait! My jade bracelet's gone!

EMPEROR [*obviously aware of the ruse*]: Let me have Wang Shang help. [*He calls towards offstage left.*] Send Wang Shang.

VOICE [*offstage*]: Send Wang Shang!

[WANG *appears at once and kneels.*]

EMPEROR: Somewhere here Lady Chên has lost a jade bracelet. Please make a thorough search.

WANG: Aye.

DOWAGER [*turned and eyeing the* EMPEROR, *but addressing* LI]: Li, dear fellow, have someone help him. We may come across a number of things.

LI: Aye. [*He shouts.*] Have Ts'ui come help look for the bracelet!

TS'UI [*entering also from the left*]: Aye!

LI: Ts'ui, dear fellow, make a thorough search for a bracelet.

TS'UI: Aye.

[*Exeunt the* DOWAGER, LI, *the* EMPEROR, *and* LADY CHÊN. TS'UI *paces, eyeing the ground along the railing.* WANG *scans the area around the bench.*]

TS'UI: Aren't they just making fools of us? Hunting for a jade bracelet here?

WANG: Bracelet or no bracelet, if the masters order us to search, we have to search.

TS'UI: Don't try talking that way to me. Whatever master gives you orders, do you think this concerns me?

WANG: We're both in the emperor's service, and he gives us our wages. It's up to us to do as he says, no matter what you say about *masters*.

TS'UI [*with a sneer*]: You can't open your mouth without saying, 'Emperor this' and 'Emperor that', but you needn't think just saying *emperor* can scare me.

WANG [*with composure and continuing to scan the ground thoroughly*]: No more nonsense now. Our business is to find that bracelet.

TS'UI [*muttering as he scuffs along by the railing*]: I get my wages from Old Buddha. Nobody can scare me. Why should I be afraid of the emperor?

WANG [*now finally annoyed*]: Don't always be flaring up. Can't we talk without dragging in our masters?

TS'UI: Look who's talking? You're the one who started this *masters* business. You mentioned him to try to rile me up, and now you say I started it.

WANG [*composure regained*]: All right. All right. Let's not squabble. All right?

TS'UI [*still growling and grubbing along the railing*]: Wait and see what's all right. Let's see how many more days there'll be for your master to be an emperor.

[WANG *straightens up abruptly, about to rebuke* TS'UI, *but then both turn their heads towards the sound of light footsteps from downstage left.*]

WANG: Who's there?

[LADY CHÊN, *noticeably out of breath, appears within the starlit area. Startled,* WANG *and* TS'UI *stare for a moment before they bow.*]

CHÊN: Have you found the bracelet?

WANG and TS'UI: No. Not yet.

CHÊN: Ts'ui, do you know where the empress is?

TS'UI: She's at the Azure Cloud Cottage.

CHÊN: Why isn't she accompanying the empress dowager? The

emperor is afraid, for the empress's sake, and urges me to try to find her. Don't bother any more about the bracelet, but do locate her quickly.

TS'UI: Aye! [*Prompt exit, right.*]

[LADY CHÊN *appears about to follow him off, right; but then, after watching to confirm his departure, she slips the bracelet from her purse, hands it to* WANG, *and addresses him rapidly.*]

CHÊN: Here's the bracelet. I didn't lose it. As soon as I've gone back, you come bring it to me. By then the emperor will have his order to K'ang Yu-wei signed and hidden in his boot. When you come, the emperor will say his boot hurts and ask you to take the sand out of it. Take out the signed order and find some way to get it safely into the city and to K'ang Yu-wei, so that he can escape at once.

WANG [*nodding*]: Aye! Aye!

CHÊN: Be careful!

WANG: Aye!

[*As* LADY CHÊN *departs hastily, left,* WANG, *looking haggard and worried, stands examining the bracelet.*]

[Lights dim out rapidly. Total darkness.]

93

The Monkey Dream

Time: September 20, 1898, about 4 a.m.
Place: a passageway adjoining the Glorious Hall of the Attained
Purity Palace.

Diffuse light makes barely visible downstage an area representing a
passageway. Upstage centre is the entrance to the Glorious Hall, but
the door is covered with a heavy curtain. Directly downstage centre
rise two pillars supporting roof-eaves. To the left high wide shutters
flank an exit leading outside the palace. To the right, stairs with
a railing appear to lead to an area within the building.

Light slightly increases as Wang Shang, carrying a gauze lantern,
enters softly, left. He is alert and anxious. Sun Te, also carrying a
gauze lantern, steps in almost at once, also from the left.

SUN: Hui-hui has just come in from the city. He says K'ang Yu-wei
eluded Jung-lu and has gotten safely aboard a steamer out of
Tientsin.
WANG: He's sure? Heaven be thanked. Our emperor can now once
more take heart.
SUN: If I hadn't galloped the whole way, going into the city that
night, K'ang would never have made it.
WANG: Yes, Sun Te, everything is a close call these days. And now
the emperor will be here any minute. Is everything taken care of?
SUN: Practically.
WANG: What about the guards on the west side?
SUN: Taken care of.
WANG: You'd better check again. If any word leaks out, you know
it's our heads to pay.

94

SUN: I know. [*Rapid exit, left.*]

[*After looking at his pocket watch,* WANG *puts his head outside, addressing an offstage attendant.*]

WANG: It's time, now.

VOICE [*from outside*]: Everything's ready.

[*Immediately footsteps sound on the stairs at the right.* WANG *turns, brushing at his clothes and standing erect. The* EMPEROR *appears on the stairs. From lack of sleep his face is heavy and his eyelids are swollen.* WANG, *taking one step forward, kneels and then stands up.*]

WANG: May fortune be kind, Emperor.

EMPEROR: Is everything taken care of?

WANG: Every precaution.

EMPEROR: How long have Yüan Shih-k'ai and Lin Hsü been waiting?

WANG: They've just come. They're waiting outside the palace.

EMPEROR: Hmn.

WANG: Allow me to report to Your Majesty, just now the eunuch Hui-hui arrived back from the city, saying that K'ang Yu-wei reached Tientsin and is safely aboard ship. Jung-lu did not catch up with him.

EMPEROR [*putting his hand to his forehead as though to impress this news*]: Are you sure? No doubt about it?

WANG: Your slave does not lie.

[SUN TE *appears, left. Seeing the* EMPEROR, *he steps forward, kneels, and then stands.*]

SUN: May fortune be kind, Emperor.

EMPEROR: Have you taken every precaution, both inside and outside the palace?

SUN: Every precaution.

EMPEROR: This is crucial. No one but our own people is to be allowed either inside the palace or near it. Be alert every moment.

SUN: Aye!

EMPEROR [*indicating, by a slight turn of the head, the curtained door, upstage centre*]: Today I am ascending the throne.

SUN: May I report to Your Majesty that Lady Chên is waiting out there beyond the door-screen. She wishes to see the emperor on urgent business.

EMPEROR [*manifestly alarmed*]: Urgent? Have her come here quickly.

SUN: Aye! [*Exit.*]

95

EMPEROR [*his face showing acute fear*]: These past two days my heart has been thudding and my muscles twitching. Does it mean that I will be . . .

WANG [*interrupting*]: Your Majesty has had no sleep and too many worries.

SUN [*entering and kneeling*]: I announce Lady Chên.

[LADY CHÊN *enters left and kneels.*]

CHÊN: May fortune be kind, Emperor.

[*The* EMPEROR *extends his hand to help her to her feet.*]

EMPEROR: K'ang Yu-wei is aboard ship and safely off.

CHÊN [*without expression*]: Your maid-slave has heard this news.

EMPEROR [*anxiously*]: What has happened now?

CHÊN [*looking about*]: Are there any outsiders around?

EMPEROR: None. Our men are on guard inside and out. You can speak freely.

CHÊN: Your maid-slave dares not speak.

EMPEROR: Come, be brave. It's all right.

CHÊN [*slowly*]: Your maid-slave – last night –

EMPEROR: Last night – what?

CHÊN: Last night . . .

EMPEROR [*urging*]: Say it!

CHÊN: Last night, a dream . . .

EMPEROR [*with relief*]: Oh, now! I thought you really had some urgent business.

CHÊN: Your maid-slave knows that a bad dream is not always a bad omen – but, all the same, this dream was a strange dream.

EMPEROR: What was your dream about?

CHÊN [*speaking as in a trance*]: Your maid-slave dreamed that she was watching Your Majesty play with a monkey.

EMPEROR [*amused*]: Was this really so strange?

CHÊN: Your maid-slave was somewhere out in the wilds. Over here a tree. Over there, a goat and a pack of dogs. Then a huge black bear – and a monkey. Standing under that tree, Your Majesty put a red hat on the monkey and helped it climb on the goat's back. [CHÊN *now shows sheer terror.*] Then suddenly the monkey climbed onto your back [CHÊN *gestures now, as she continues*] and fastened a chain around your neck and chained you to the tree. While you were struggling, the bear clawed at your legs. [CHÊN *is now crying and her voice strains.*] Then the goat drove at you with his horns

96

and gashed your chest and you began to bleed. I tried to save you. Then the goat drove at me and its horns gashed and pierced. There was a sharp pain in my heart. I cried, 'Help!' The pain woke me up. I was drenched with sweat. I opened my eyes. The room was all dark and quiet. The only sound was just the gong for the third watch.

EMPEROR: Hmn!

CHÊN: Does it seem so dreadful to you? Or not? Even now my hair stands up when I think of it.

EMPEROR [*comforting her*]: Any bad dream is dreadful, of course. But just put it out of your mind and all will be well.

CHÊN: [*abruptly*]: But isn't Your Majesty going to see Yüan Shih-k'ai today?

EMPEROR: I'm about to see him this minute.

CHÊN: Your Majesty – please – do not see him.

EMPEROR: Why not?

CHÊN: Your maid-slave has perceived that this man cannot be trusted.

EMPEROR [*lightly*]: Only a few days ago, when I interviewed him at the Benevolent Long Life Palace, you studied him for a long time from behind your screen. After he left, you said he appeared to be quite unusual. So why now do you insist that he cannot be trusted?

CHÊN: To inquire into competence when making appointments is Your Majesty's business. Since your maid-slave would not wish to interfere, she said nothing further.

EMPEROR: Then why do you speak only now?

CHÊN [*lowering her head*]: Now . . .

EMPEROR: Feel free to speak.

CHÊN [*weeping*]: This evil dream, I fear, is not a good omen.

EMPEROR: But what has your dream to do with Yüan Shih-k'ai?

CHÊN: His surname is *Yüan*.

EMPEROR: But what . . .?

CHÊN: In my dream, the creature who put a chain around your neck was a *yüan*, a *monkey*!

EMPEROR [*now manifestly a little worried himself but keeping up the pretence of merely teasing her*]: In that case, Lin Hsü, who is also waiting outside, should be in that dream also. I suppose he is the *lin-tree* of your dream. What about that *goat*? My chief supporters in the reform plans are Yang Shen-hsiu and Yang Jui. This seems to make two *yang* – two *goats*.

CHÊN [*pleading*]: This is why your maid-slave is in such dread. Your Majesty, please make up your mind now – please do not see Yüan Shih-k'ai.

EMPEROR: But we have serious business. I must see Yüan Shih-k'ai and Lin Hsü – and now, at once.

CHÊN [*kneeling*]: Your Majesty!

EMPEROR [*distraught*]: Well, let me see Lin Hsü first. After I've seen him, I'll come talk with you again. [*He helps* LADY CHÊN *to her feet.*]

CHÊN: Thank you, Your Majesty.

EMPEROR [*speaking towards the left exit, to attendants outside*]: I am now about to ascend the throne.

WANG and SUN [*offstage*]: The emperor is coming!

[WANG *and* SUN *now hurry in, adjust the* EMPEROR'*s robes, and stand at attention as the* EMPEROR *goes out, left.*]

WANG [*to* SUN]: Be a good fellow, Sun, and bring a chair here for Lady Chên.

[CHÊN *nods appreciatively but says nothing.*]

SUN: Certainly.

[*As* SUN *leaves, right, below the staircase, an offstage voice, left, becomes audible.*]

VOICE [*off-stage*]: Lin Hsü is asked to come up.

CHÊN [*to* WANG]: When Sun returns, you and Sun both go stand by the curtain [*indicating the curtain upstage centre*] and listen to what Lin Hsü says – and report to me.

WANG: Aye!

[*As* SUN TE *arrives with the chair and* LADY CHÊN *seats herself,* WANG *moves softly up to the curtain.*]

CHÊN [*to* SUN]: I've heard that Old Buddha is coming back to the city this morning, early. Is she really coming?

SUN: Yes, she is. The emperor is to meet her at eight this morning, at the Ying-hsiu gate.

CHÊN: Hmn!

SUN: These last several days there have been lots of rumours. I've heard it said that, once Old Buddha is inside the city, there'll be plenty of bad business.

CHÊN: But K'ang Yu-wei's gone. What is she up to now?

SUN: K'ang Yu-wei's gone. But there's still Yang Shen-hsiu and

Lin Hsü, and there's T'an Ssu-t'ung, Yang Jui, and Liu Kuang-ti. There's also Chang Yin-huan and Li Tuan-fen. They're all still in the city and can't get away.

CHÊN: You mean that Old Buddha plans to arrest them all?

SUN: Your slave dares not say.

[WANG *approaches.*]

WANG [*to* SUN]: Now you go listen.

[SUN *takes his place by the curtain.*]

CHÊN: What is Lin Hsü saying?

WANG [*kneeling*]: May I report to my lady that the situation is very unfavourable.

CHÊN [*standing up abruptly and walking about*]: How do you mean?

WANG: He's saying that the dowager is furious about the escape of K'ang Yu-wei, that she's coming to the city to scoop up all her enemies in one net, that she'll arrest everybody and have everybody killed or banished.

CHÊN [*urgently*]: And what else is Lin Hsü saying?

WANG: He says he's found out that Old Buddha's going to make Jung-lu the grand councillor for Peking, that she's going to lock up the emperor, and she's going to take over full charge of state affairs again.

CHÊN: And hearing all this, what is the emperor saying?

WANG: First the emperor asked, 'Have you been discussing what's to be done now?' and Lin Hsü replied, 'Obviously the new and the old cannot control the same powers in the same territory, and your ministers advise you to cease being so cautious. The empress dowager is going to be ruthless, so Your Majesty had best follow the saying "Measure your way by your rival's measure, make your opponent's tactics your tactics".'

CHÊN: Hmn! And the emperor replied?

WANG: The emperor asked how he proposed to proceed in using the opponent's tactics.

CHÊN: And Lin Hsü said?

WANG [*rising to exchange places with* SUN]: At that point I came to report to you.

SUN [*kneeling*]: May I report to my lady that Lin Hsü has been saying that the situation is very critical and that His Majesty must act at once – and then he mentioned Yüan Shih-k'ai.

CHÊN [*sharply*]: What about Yüan Shih-k'ai?

SUN [*speaking with increasing rapidity*]: Lin says that Yüan Shih-k'ai has been assigned to train the new army at Tientsin, that he is not opposed to the reform, that he has plenty of courage. When I stopped listening, Lin Hsü was just asking the emperor to trust Yüan Shih-k'ai, because of his loyalty . . .

CHÊN [*to herself*]: Yüan Shih-k'ai, his loyalty . . .

[SUN *and* WANG *change places again.*]

WANG: Reporting to my lady . . .

CHÊN [*abruptly*]: What is Lin Hsü trusting Yüan Shih-k'ai to undertake?

WANG [*speaking at top-speed*]: To kill Jung-lu at the governor-general's office, to bring ten thousand soldiers by train to Peking the same day, to surround the Summer Palace, to force the empress dowager to surrender all authority. She is to be allowed to keep on living at the Summer Palace but no longer to meddle in affairs of state.

CHÊN [*tensely*]: Has the emperor agreed?

WANG [*rising to change places with* SUN]: At that point I came to report to you.

SUN [*kneeling*]: My lady, the emperor says he is afraid that, with the empress dowager coming into the city today, a *coup d'état* is already underway.

CHÊN [*startled*]: No!

SUN: So Lin Hsü says, 'All the more reason why Your Majesty should act at once. Send Yüan Shih-k'ai by train now to Tientsin to carry out our plan.'

[*As* WANG *and* SUN *change places once again, rifle fire resounds from somewhere outside.*]

WANG [*kneeling*]: The interview is over.

CHÊN: What did the emperor say?

[*Just as* WANG *opens his mouth to answer, the* EMPEROR *himself appears, coming through the rear throne-curtain.* WANG *and* SUN *promptly bow and exit.*]

EMPEROR: Lin Hsü has just been telling me . . .

CHÊN: Your maid-slave already knows. Has Your Majesty agreed?

EMPEROR [*firmly*]: Of course I have.

CHÊN: But, Emperor, the risks?

EMPEROR: In this crisis whoever acts first has the advantage. I have no alternative.

CHÊN: But to entrust this to Yüan Shih-k'ai? Suppose Yüan turns against you? Won't this make matters even worse?

EMPEROR: I feel much the same confidence in Yüan as I have in Li Hung-chang. Yüan is dignified and sincere. I cannot picture him as the mean sort who would betray, for his own advantage, the man he has sworn to serve.

CHÊN: Your maid-slave remembers that, with all his dignity, Yüan doesn't look you straight in the eye – and so it seems to me that, in a crisis, he may not be dependable.

EMPEROR: Well, I propose to assure him to his own advantage too. When he completes this . . . assignment – , I'll appoint him governor-general of Chihli.

CHÊN [*resuming the strained and frantic tones in which she earlier recounted her dream*]: Your Majesty must not rely on Yüan! He'll clamp that chain around your neck!

EMPEROR [*mildly impatient*]: I've always admired you for being astute, but today, it seems, you are merely childish.

CHÊN [*imploring*]: But – the dream – last night –

EMPEROR: At this juncture I can't alter major decisions on account of your dreams.

CHÊN [*kneeling*]: Your maid-slave begs Your Majesty to reconsider.

EMPEROR [*lifting her up*]: Enough of this. The decision is made. Succeed or fail, live or die, now only Heaven determines. [*He addresses attendants who are off-stage left.*] Have Yüan Shih-k'ai come up.

VOICE [*off-stage*]: Aye!

CHÊN: Well then, will Your Majesty at least agree to see him right here?

EMPEROR: Why here?

CHÊN: Your maid-slave is still uneasy, and here she could observe him once more.

EMPEROR: Can't you watch him through the throne-curtain?

CHÊN: If I have to stay out of sight behind the throne-curtain, I can't see him clearly.

EMPEROR: Very well, I'll see him here. [*He speaks to the outside attendants.*] Ask Yüan Shih-k'ai to step in here.

VOICE [*off-stage*]: Aye! Request that Yüan Shih-k'ai come directly here.

CHÊN [*with a slight bow*]: Thank you, Your Majesty.

[CHÊN *steps quickly into the shadows at the side of the staircase. The* EMPEROR *seats himself formally in the chair which* SUN *had arranged for Lady Chên. Emerging from the rear, through the throne-curtain,* WANG *advances, carrying a cushion which he places on the floor before the* EMPEROR.]

WANG: Yüan Shih-k'ai is coming now.

[*Lantern in hand,* SUN TE, *escorting* YÜAN, *appears, entering from the left.* WANG *and* SUN *at once depart, left, and* YÜAN *kneels just a step in advance of the far-left door-screen.*]

YÜAN: Your insignificant minister, Yüan Shih-k'ai, reverently greets Your Majesty.

[YÜAN *now removes his hat, touches his forehead to the ground, rises, walks forward, and kneels on the cushion before the* EMPEROR.]

EMPEROR: I am assigning you to train the troops at Tientsin. Will you offer your loyalty to me, without reservations and without faltering?

YÜAN: Your minister affirms to the Heavenly Grace of Your Majesty that he will be loyal even though his body should be set to the rack and all his bones broken.

EMPEROR: I am carrying out reforms. Will you serve me in these reforms?

YÜAN: Reform is essential to the prosperity and strength of the nation. If Your Majesty finds that this minor official can be of service, he is happy to serve.

EMPEROR [*lowering his voice and taking a conversational tone*]: You know that the empress dowager and the conservatives object to these reforms.

YÜAN: Your minister knows to some extent about this. But now that Your Majesty has been ruler of this nation for a good number of years and your reputation as an enlightened ruler is known throughout the world, it does not appear that the empress dowager should intrude in affairs of state.

EMPEROR: But the empress dowager is determined to put an end to our reforms. What, in your opinion, should be done to bring an end to her interference?

YÜAN: Your minister remembers that in *Tso's Commentary* it is recorded that Chuang of Cheng, though he required his mother to remove to a distant city, was not castigated by the state archivists. They regarded Chuang's order as necessary for reasons of state and no offence against filial piety.

EMPEROR [*with an approving smile*]: You mean that I should follow the example of Duke Chuang of Cheng?

YÜAN: Only Your Sacred Majesty makes decisions. But your minister dares not speak idly.

EMPEROR [*speaking earnestly and intimately*]: If I propose to be guided by the precedent of Duke Chuang of Cheng, would you render me a service requiring maximum loyalty?

YÜAN [*touching his forehead to the ground*]: Even at the cost of his life your minister will serve Your Majesty, offering his life in gratitude for Your Majesty's trust.

EMPEROR [*naively pleased*]: You are truly a bulwark of my court.

YÜAN [*again kowtowing*]: Thank you, Your Majesty.

EMPEROR: What I am asking of you is a service both important and confidential. Are you willing to undertake it?

YÜAN: I do not know the nature of the confidential service to which Your Majesty refers.

EMPEROR [*removing a document from his sleeve and handing it to* YÜAN]: Examine this.

[YÜAN *takes the document and turns it to catch light from the lantern rays coming in from the left over the door-screen. After he has scanned a line or two, his hands tremble noticeably. His hands are still trembling as he completes the reading and looks up, folding the paper in his hands.*]

EMPEROR: You – can undertake this?

YÜAN [*hesitantly*]: Your minister – your minister – will try – to perform his loyal duty for you.

EMPEROR [*rising and giving his hand to* YÜAN *to help him up from the cushion*]: Performing this duty will be a major service to the nation. [*He turns his head, calling off towards the right.*] Wang Shang!

WANG [*entering and kneeling*]: Aye?

EMPEROR: Bring the writing case, my jade seal, and also a small gold arrow.

WANG: Aye! [*Exit, right.*]

EMPEROR [*addressing* YÜAN *face to face*]: Jung-lu now controls the Peiyang Army and is, as you know, one of the dowager's closest and most trusted advisers. I am appointing you as an imperial commissioner. I am also giving you an autograph decree and a gold arrow. Take the first train this morning to Tientsin. As soon as you have killed Jung-lu, you are at once in possession of your appointment as governor-general of Chihli. You are then immediately to transfer ten thousand of the New Army men to

Peking, also to proceed to surround the Summer Palace and hold siege there until the empress dowager surrenders all her claims to power. These are heavy responsibilities. Proceed with discretion. [WANG *enters, right, carrying on a tray the writing materials, the seal, and the gold arrow.*]

YÜAN: Your minister complies with the imperial mandate.

EMPEROR: Good.

[*The* EMPEROR *seats himself again and* WANG, *kneeling before him, holds the tray. The* EMPEROR *writes a decree rapidly, stamps it with his seal, and takes the gold arrow from the tray.* WANG *exits swiftly, carrying the tray.* YÜAN *kneels, and the* EMPEROR *hands him the decree.*]

EMPEROR: Yüan Shih-k'ai, can you serve me loyally and without swerving?

YÜAN: Your minister devotes himself to Your Majesty wholly, to death and beyond.

EMPEROR [*his voice trembling with earnestness and anxiety*]: My life, my nation, everything now depends upon you. [*He holds up the gold arrow.*] This arrow is not to be carried lightly. With it you carry the power to put to death any major official whose death is deemed necessary. Given this trust, do not fail me.

YÜAN: Your Majesty may set his heart at rest.

[*The* EMPEROR *is about to place the arrow in* YÜAN'*s hand but then hesitates.*]

EMPEROR: Not because I do not trust you but because the responsibility is heavy, will you swear before Heaven?

[YÜAN *shows a flicker of dismay but then at once regains composure.*]

YÜAN: Your Majesty, your minister will swear before Heaven. [*On the kneeling cushion,* YÜAN *turns to face outwards – towards the audience – raising his eyes; the movement of his eyes, fully visible to the audience though not to the* EMPEROR, *suggests doubts and lack of conviction.*] August Heaven is above me. If I, Yüan Shih-k'ai, fail this great trust placed in me by the emperor, later – may anxiety and misfortunes bring my death.

EMPEROR [*handing over the arrow with an abrupt, thrusting motion*]: Such an oath is mighty.

YÜAN: We should act at once. Your minister should now proceed. [*He kowtows, and the* EMPEROR *extends his hand to help him rise.*]

EMPEROR: In this crucial business, be bold – and wary.

YÜAN [*bowing*]: Your minister complies with the imperial mandate.

EMPEROR [*calling towards off-stage left*]: Now, before the sun comes up, escort Minister Yüan from the palace.

VOICE [*off-stage*]: Aye! [SUN TE, *holding his lantern, appears from around the door-screen.*]

EMPEROR: We shall be awaiting word of the successful outcome of your mission.

YÜAN: At earliest, today – at latest, tomorrow morning – your minister will again report to you here in Peking.

[YÜAN *bows deeply and exits left, followed by* SUN TE. *At once* LADY CHÊN *emerges from the shadows at the right, and the* EMPEROR *turns towards her.*]

EMPEROR [*taking both of* CHÊN'*s hands in his own*]: Now your heart should be at rest.

CHÊN: But when Yüan Shih-k'ai accepted your decree, your maid-slave observed that he was uneasy and his expression raised doubts. Your maid-slave's heart is not at rest.

EMPEROR [*sternly*]: Why these stubborn suspicions? The loyalty of Yüan Shih-k'ai, his valour – they are all evident in his words and in his face. You heard him swear to Heaven. If you won't trust a man like him, whom would you trust?

CHÊN: Your maid-slave can only pray that Heaven grant Your Majesty a favourable outcome.

[LADY CHÊN *looks up at him as though to ask a question, then bursts into tears and buries her face in her hands.*]

EMPEROR: It seems to me that you are not very well today – probably because you have had no sleep. You had best go rest awhile.

CHÊN: As you say. [*She starts towards the door-screen at the left but then turns and kneels.*] Emperor, when Yüan Shih-k'ai reaches Tientsin, suppose that, to save himself, he betrays all your plans to Jung-lu, sends Jung-lu to Peking with the troops, lets Jung-lu report everything to the empress dowager at the Summer Palace – and then they arrest everyone who is pledged to you and come seize Your Majesty also. Perhaps, Your Majesty, the monkey is already clamping the chain around your neck?

EMPEROR [*impatiently*]: You and your bad dreams! If I were to follow your way of thinking, would we ever finish making our oar?
[CHÊN'*s head droops.*]

[Lights out, rapidly.]

$\mathcal{H}$ ACT III

FIRST SCENE
Coup d'État

Time: September 21, 1898, about 5.30 a.m.
Place: throne-room of the Central Harmony Palace.

Light illuminates only the centre of the stage, showing a throne-platform, throne-chair, and small, brocade-covered table upstage right of centre. Behind the throne-platform hangs a heavily embroidered curtain. Slightly to the left, at floor level, stands a portable screen marking an entrance area from the rear of the room. Tall window shutters, just beyond this door-screen, let in thin lines of light, as of the sky just before dawn. A single tall candle in a heavy stand burns at each of the front corners of the throne-platform.

Wang Shang, carrying a gauze lantern and a documents box, emerges from behind the screen and is immediately followed by the emperor, who walks slowly and heavily, and appears even more haggard than during the final scene of Act II. He seems about to step to the platform but then turns and addresses Wang.

EMPEROR [*his voice tense*]: Still no news?

WANG: None. Your slave has already reminded the others that any news they hear should be reported at once.

EMPEROR [*pacing about restlessly*]: With Yüan Shih-k'ai gone a whole day now, why is there no news at all?

WANG: Knowing Your Majesty's anxiety, your slave has sent two private couriers into the city to find out what they can. They should be back very soon now.

EMPEROR [*lifting his head sharply*]: Hmn!

WANG: Meanwhile, will Your Majesty examine the paper submitted by the Ministry of Ceremonies regarding the sacrificial offerings to be made to the gods of the land and crops?

106

EMPEROR: I suppose I should.

[*The* EMPEROR *seats himself in the throne-chair. Bowing,* WANG *places the documents box on the table, bows again, and exits. The* EMPEROR *reaches towards the box but then pauses and stares into space. Recovering himself, he finally opens the box and begins to scan reports. Rapid footsteps rear catch his attention and, letting the papers lie unread, he sits listening. He shoves the papers back into the box and stands up as* SUN TE *bursts in, breathing heavily.* SUN TE *is immediately followed by* WANG SHANG.]

SUN [*kneeling*]: Emperor – may – fortune be kind!

EMPEROR: News?

SUN [*remaining on his knees*]: Report to Your Majesty, the news – is – very – bad.

EMPEROR: Speak up! Quickly!

SUN: The guards surrounding the Forbidden City here are all new men!

EMPEROR: What's this? Who are they?

SUN: New troops from Tientsin.

EMPEROR [*torn between hope and suspicion*]: New troops – from Tientsin . . .

SUN: They took over a little after two o'clock this morning.

EMPEROR: Ordered to Peking by Yüan Shih-k'ai?

SUN: It's said they're under the command of Governor-General Jung-lu.

EMPEROR [*stunned*]: Jung-lu!

SUN: Your slave understands that they are all Jung-lu's men.

EMPEROR: Jung-lu – he has come to Peking?

SUN: He is here. It's said he arrived in Peking yesterday afternoon around five o'clock.

EMPEROR [*to* WANG]: Why wasn't I informed?

WANG [*kneeling*]: Your slave deserves death – but none of us heard anything at all about this.

EMPEROR [*heavily*]: Then Yüan Shih-k'ai was struck down by Jung-lu. [*He addresses* SUN.] And what has Jung-lu been doing since he came into Peking?

SUN: Your slave has not been able to find out anything further.

EMPEROR: No other information at all?

SUN: None at all.

EMPEROR: Send more of our men to scout out news and keep the reports coming in promptly.

SUN [*standing and about to depart*]: Aye!

EMPEROR: Hold on!

SUN [*kneeling again*]: Aye.

EMPEROR: Send private couriers to warn Yang Shen-hsiu, T'an Ssu-t'ung, Lin Hsü, Yang Jui, and Liu Kuang-ti, telling them to try to get out of the city at once.

SUN: Aye.

[SUN *dashes out,* WANG *following him. Stepping down from his chair, the* EMPEROR *prowls about aimlessly, tensing his hands and beating with his fists on his head and chest.*]

EMPEROR: Why didn't I listen to her! Now Yüan Shih-k'ai really has me and everything's done for. Jung-lu's certainly reached the dowager by this time. Now what? Now what?

[WANG SHANG *enters.*]

WANG [*kneeling*]: Lady Chên wishes to see Your Majesty. Urgent.

EMPEROR: Have her come in. [WANG *hurries out.*] Perhaps she has already heard.

[WANG *re-enters, with* LADY CHÊN.]

LADY CHÊN [*kneeling*]: Emperor, may fortune be kind.

EMPEROR [*helping her to rise*]: Up now, quickly.

CHÊN: Your Majesty knows that Jung-lu has brought his troops into Peking?

EMPEROR: This I've learned just a few moments ago.

CHÊN: Also just a few moments ago, just as the sun was coming up, Hsiao Hsi-lu, one of Old Buddha's palace girls in the hair-dressing section, managed to reach your maid-slave with the news. She tells me that, just after five yesterday afternoon, Jung-lu, in ordinary streetclothes, rushed into the Yi-luan Palace, reached the dowager, kowtowed and wept, and begged the dowager to protect him – and then the dowager sent everyone away except Jung-lu and Li Lien-ying.

EMPEROR: What did Jung-lu tell the dowager?

CHÊN: The girl does not know, just says the dowager went white and sent everyone out – and then sent Li Lien-ying out too – and orders were given for all her advisors to come to the palace, Prince Li, Kang-i, Yü-lu, Wang Wen-shao, Huai-ta-pu, Hsü Ying-k'uei, Hsü T'ung, and Prince Ch'ing – and they all came except Prince Ch'ing, who is ill.

EMPEROR [*astounded*]: With all this going on and we hear nothing – it seems all of us must have been in a trance.

CHÊN: The girl says that the dowager had Li Lien-ying set a watch on everyone, so that none of the eunuchs and none of the girls could get out of the palace all night.

EMPEROR: Anything further?

CHÊN: After the conference the dowager sent the advisors away but, at two in the morning, she issued orders deploying the regular guards around the Forbidden City to other posts and installing Jung-lu's troops – but the girl doesn't know how much earlier Jung-lu's troops may have arrived in Peking.

EMPEROR [*tonelessly*]: So we're now fish set to broil.

CHÊN: More nearly perhaps, say the chain is around your neck. Your Majesty should try to escape at once.

EMPEROR: But I can't just run off!

CHÊN: Jung-lu's troops do not know you by sight, and Your Majesty could still slip out.

EMPEROR: But even if I managed to get outside the Forbidden City, where would I go?

CHÊN: The southeastern provinces are still supporting you. Take a train to Tientsin, Your Majesty, a steamer to Shanghai, and then go on to Nanking. From Nanking call in Liu K'un-i, Governor-General of Liang-Kiang, and some of the other major officials. Issue a proclamation, say that the empress dowager, to impede the reforms, brought Jung-lu's troops to Peking to seize the government. When the people in general and the officials and the merchants learn what has really happened, they'll rise up on your behalf and you'll have them with you forever. This is our best hope. Your maid-slave begs Your Majesty to proceed at once. [*She kneels.*]

EMPEROR [*lifting her up*]: But this would involve far too many risks.

CHÊN: Any more risks than Your Majesty takes by remaining here?

EMPEROR: We're in danger. I know. But whatever I do, the responsibility is mine, and I can't dodge it by running off.

CHÊN: If you don't go now while there's a chance, all you've tried to achieve these past three months goes for nothing – and now your life is at stake. Surely Your Majesty knows the fury and ruthlessness of the empress dowager?

EMPEROR: But even suppose I went to Nanking, what could I do from there?

CHÊN: Your Majesty will be supported and defended by Liu K'un-i and by Li Hung-chang and by many other major officials and will also have the good will of the people. How could the empress dowager reach you then?

EMPEROR: Perhaps she wouldn't be able to reach me in Nanking, but that doesn't mean she will give up her power. She and the conservatives might very likely set up another emperor, and then the most I could do would be to maintain a rival capital in Nanking and so split the empire. This country, once divided, will be even easier prey for the foreigners, capturing one section and then another. [*He sucks in his breath sharply.*] I'd rather give up my life, at this point, than divide the empire.

[LADY CHÊN *is impressed by his argument and looks at him with respect and affection.*]

CHÊN: Your Majesty carries in his heart the welfare of the whole nation. [*She tenses her lips and nostrils to hold back tears.*] What more can your maid-slave say?

EMPEROR: Only that now we may very likely be separated forever.

CHÊN [*shocked*]: Your Majesty! Your maid-slave long ago gave her heart to you, to share everything with you, even death.

EMPEROR [*with a wry smile*]: No! No, in this you must not become involved. You must get away at once.

CHÊN [*pleading*]: Does Your Majesty suppose that your maid-slave fears death, that she cares about saving her own life?

EMPEROR: No, it's not that. I do not think that. But why should you have to suffer because I do? Isn't it enough that I shall be made to pay?

CHÊN: But your maid-slave chooses –

EMPEROR [*interrupting*]: Impossible! You know very well that, for the dowager, you've always been a nail in her eye, that she's never had any use for you. Can't you imagine what she'll contrive for you now?

CHÊN [*calmly*]: What can she do? The worst she can do is put me to death.

EMPEROR: It's not just a matter of dying or not dying. What I'm afraid of is that she'll put you away in some hole and torture you, not just hurt you physically but try to drive you mad, insult you, berate you, whip you, sneer at you. You've always led a protected life, and you can't endure even an insulting word. How could you endure the tortures she'll think up? [*He takes her hands.*] You must go, get away, flee – at once.

CHÊN: I am not leaving.

EMPEROR: Listen, you must. Get away at once – or it may be too late.

CHÊN: But, Your Majesty, what about you?

EMPEROR: I've long since stopped worrying about myself, my life or death.

CHÊN [*weeping*]: If Your Majesty intends to sacrifice himself for the empire, can't you let your maid-slave sacrifice herself for her husband?

EMPEROR [*urgently*]: I beg of you, please try to escape now, at once.

CHÊN [*kneeling*]: Let me beg of you, Your Majesty. Let me remain here.

EMPEROR [*trying to drag her to her feet and, when she resists, shouting at her*]: Go now! Go! At once!

CHÊN: Unless we go together . . .

[*The* EMPEROR's *face is torn with anguish. He clutches at her hands.*]

CHÊN: Do you remember our small boat? [*She speaks eagerly.*] Let's go now, together. For my sake – and for the sake of the empire. Now!

EMPEROR [*gathering her in his arms*]: Our empire . . .

[*At this moment footsteps resound beyond the door-screen. The* EMPEROR *and* LADY CHÊN *turn their heads towards the sound. The* EMPRESS DOWAGER *steps in. With abrupt firm steps she advances towards them. She is followed by* LI LIEN-YING, TS'UI YÜ-KUEI, *four other eunuchs, and two palace girls, all of whom, except for* LI LIEN-YING, *simply enter the room, cross in front of the door-screen, and go out again. As the* EMPRESS DOWAGER *advances, her mouth grim, her eyes fixed and staring, the* EMPEROR *and* LADY CHÊN *bow.*]

EMPEROR: May fortune be kind, Imperial Parent.

CHÊN: May fortune be kind, Empress Dowager.

DOWAGER [*ignoring them and addressing* LI LIEN-YING]: Bring me a chair!

LI [*as he goes out*]: Aye.

EMPEROR [*gesturing towards the platform*]: Imperial Parent, will you go up to the throne?

DOWAGER [*mocking*]: How could I dare? [*As* LI *now enters, carrying a chair and a yellow satin chair-cover, the* DOWAGER *indicates, by a toss of her head, that he is to place it to the right, below the platform. She addresses him.*] Put it there! [*Then, as* LI, *having set down the chair and covered it with the satin, starts to leave, she addresses him again.*] Hold on! You have not even saluted the emperor and Lady Chên. Do you want to lose your head perhaps?

LI: Thank you, Old Buddha, for reminding your slave. [*He bows, one knee bent, arm extended.*] May fortune be kind, Emperor. May fortune be kind, Lady Chên.

[LI *now takes up position at the right side of the door-screen.* LADY CHÊN *also steps back, moving towards the left side of the screen. The* DOWAGER *is seated. The* EMPEROR *kneels.*]

EMPEROR: Imperial Parent, you have come to give instructions to your son?

DOWAGER: I come to greet you and to ask you to save my life. The emperor certainly knows why I have come.

EMPEROR [*firmly*]: Your minister would not dare.

DOWAGER [*her face distorted by both fear and fury*]: You would not dare! Why did you send Yüan Shih-k'ai to murder me?

EMPEROR: Your minister did not send Yüan Shih-k'ai to disturb the Imperial Parent.

DOWAGER [*taking the emperor's decree and the gold arrow from her sleeve*]: What are these? Will you still try to deny this? [*At the word* this, *she flings the gold arrow on the floor at the knees of the* EMPEROR.]

EMPEROR: Your minister ordered Yüan to kill Jung-lu but gave no orders to disturb the Imperial Parent.

DOWAGER: You did not order him to murder me? What orders did you give him?

EMPEROR: Your minister ordered him to lead the New Army into Peking, to wipe out the rebels, to protect the imperial family, to clean up the court administration.

DOWAGER [*tapping the document*]: Here are the words of your decree. But tell me, what oral instructions did you give him?

EMPEROR [*continuing his same calm and open manner*]: Your minister instructed Yüan, after reaching Peking, to go on to surround the Summer Palace and secure from the Imperial Parent the surrender of all political authority and to assure the Imperial Parent that she would be protected to enjoy the rest of her life among the hills and waters of the Summer Palace. Yüan Shih-k'ai received no orders to murder the Imperial Parent.

DOWAGER: So you sugar your malice with sweet words! [*She grinds her teeth and, in mounting fury, she grips the decree and reads from it.*] '. . . to enjoy the rest of life among the hills and waters of the Summer Palace.' [*She screams the following words, full voice.*] Doesn't this mean you intended to drive me to my death – of despair?

[*The* EMPRESS DOWAGER'*s face, twitching and distorted, shows both wrath and genuine terror. She is trembling. It is clear that she is, in her own way, thoroughly shaken and miserable and, this time, not merely playing with anger for its effect.*]

EMPEROR [*touching his forehead to the floor*]: Your minister would never dare.

DOWAGER [*stern, but according to her own view of herself, sincere*]: Have you really forgotten all my great concern for you?

EMPEROR [*abashed*]: How could your minister forget your great concern, Imperial Parent?

DOWAGER: I took you into the palace when you were five years old and I made you emperor. Now you are twenty-seven. I and only I gave you your prerogatives. I selected an empress for you. I even conceded to your authority over state affairs. Now in your ingratitude, you undertake reforms by following the advice of rebellious officials and ignoring the instructions of our ancestors. But even this is not enough. Now in my old age you want to destroy what life I have left. [*She speaks slowly and earnestly.*] Do you have any conscience at all?

EMPEROR [*again kowtowing*]: Your minister deserves to be put to death.

DOWAGER [*abruptly savage once more*]: How fortunate it is that it is not fated for me to die yet awhile! [*She resumes her characteristically cynical smile.*] In your blindness you chose the wrong emissary. You thought Yüan Shih-k'ai's loyalty was to you. [*The* EMPEROR'*s head drops and his shoulders are tense.*] Allow me to inform you that he sold you the moment he arrived in Tientsin.

EMPEROR [*his head jerking up, his face drawn*]: The dream, then – was truly an omen. He has sold me – and the reform.

DOWAGER: When I gave my consent to the reform, I did not realize you would also become so insolent as not even to tolerate my existence.

EMPEROR: It is not true that your minister cannot tolerate the existence of the Imperial Parent, but . . .

DOWAGER [*cutting in*]: But! But who is it, then, who cannot tolerate my existence?

EMPEROR: The Imperial Parent cannot tolerate our reform movement, but it is not the reform which cannot tolerate the Imperial Parent.

DOWAGER [*in high fury and screaming again*]: Ah! So it is the reform movement that cannot tolerate my existence! Then I will fight to the death against these reforms! [*She addresses* LI LIEN-YING.] Li, take my verbal order to the chief of the Peking police to arrest every member of the reform party, to throw them in prison under warrants from the Imperial Ministry of Correction. Don't let even one of them get away.

LI [*already leaving*]: Aye.

EMPEROR [*kowtowing*]: Imperial Parent, have mercy, spare their lives. They merely followed orders from your minister in carrying out the reforms. Your minister alone should take the blame and endure the punishment.

DOWAGER: Do not suppose it is that simple. In their insolence they have rebelled against me – and I choose to arrange their deaths – one by one.

EMPEROR [*bitterly urgent*]: Imperial Parent, you must not kill them!

DOWAGER [*coldly amused*]: I am not to be allowed to kill them?

EMPEROR: To destroy them is to destroy the most capable men now serving the Great Ch'ing dynasty. To kill them is to destroy the empire.

DOWAGER: Bah! [*Her tone is quiet but vicious.*] I would rather destroy the empire than pardon them.

EMPEROR [*looking at her warily and, perhaps for the first time, guessing that she is actually* non compos mentis]: Imperial Parent . . .

DOWAGER [*now in an intoxication of fury*]: I'll kill them, I'll kill them, and I'll let them see how I manage state affairs! They teach you about reforms and new administrations! I can destroy reforms! I can call back all your orders! So it's the foreign powers, they say, who are so powerful in this and so clever in that, and so they want to get you to cut off your braid, to get you to learn English, to make you over into a foreign devil. [*She is now shrieking.*] Ah! Ah! One of these days I'll kill every foreign devil in the

empire and then I shall be satisfied, then I shall be happy!
[*During the* DOWAGER'*s tirade the* EMPEROR, *having risen from his knees, stands quietly facing her.*]
EMPEROR: The Imperial Parent has no respect for the hardships suffered by our ancestors in acquiring this empire? You will risk letting the empire be destroyed?
DOWAGER [*now canny and contentious*]: You think you can threaten me by talking about our ancestors?
EMPEROR [*incisively*]: Imperial Parent, if you insist that all power remain in your hands, your minister is willing to abdicate – on these conditions: that the Imperial Parent consider the whole situation calmly and no longer rant and scream; and that the Imperial Parent spare the lives of our capable men and support the reforms so that the empire can once again become prosperous and powerful. If these stipulations are fulfilled, even though the Imperial Parent has her minister killed and his body torn to bits, he will hold no ill will. [*He is very earnest.*] Will the Imperial Parent agree to these stipulations, so that your minister can die with an easy heart?
DOWAGER [*taken aback*]: Who is it wants to have all this authority? You are the one who cannot tolerate this old woman and even try to take her life. And yet you accuse me of trying to take away your authority.
[LI LIEN-YING, *entering, pauses a moment to appraise the* DOWAGER'*s mood and then, advancing, kneels.*]
LI: May I report to Old Buddha that Governor-General Jung-lu, the princes, and the major officials await an audience in the Diligent Administration Hall.
DOWAGER: Very good. Let them wait. But [*with a caustic glance towards the* EMPEROR] send Jung-lu in here, alone, to see me.
[*The* EMPEROR *is visibly dismayed.*]
LI [*departing*]: Aye.
DOWAGER [*derisively*]: You've been trying to chop Jung-lu's head. When he comes in, do not neglect this excellent opportunity.
EMPEROR: Your minister does not want Jung-lu's head. He only wants the Imperial Parent to comply with the stipulations.
DOWAGER: So you want me to comply. [*She has assumed her fixed, mocking smile.*] Since you try to kill my useful men, should I not kill yours?

EMPEROR [*kneeling*]: Mercy, Imperial Parent.

DOWAGER [*emphatically*]: You want me to pardon those upstarts and support the reforms. But there will be no reforms so long as I am alive.

EMPEROR [*abruptly standing up again*]: Since the Imperial Parent shows no mercy, your minister will consider other procedures.

DOWAGER: What do you propose?

EMPEROR: To issue a decree protecting them.

DOWAGER: And I shall issue a decree chopping their heads.

[*During this interchange* LADY CHÊN *emerges from the shadows beyond the door-screen, but neither the* DOWAGER *nor the* EMPEROR *observes her.*]

EMPEROR: I am the emperor. My decrees must be obeyed. [*He turns on his heel, back to the* DOWAGER *and facing the audience.*]

DOWAGER [*sardonically*]: Ah, wonderful! It was my power which made you emperor. I have the power to depose you also!

CHÊN [*approaching and kneeling*]: May fortune be kind, Empress Dowager. The emperor is the head of the nation. The empress dowager cannot depose him by saying so. Empress Dowager, pardon the emperor.

DOWAGER [*startled*]: Who let you in here? Do you come and go as you please?

CHÊN: Your maid-slave deserves death.

DOWAGER: If I choose to depose him, I depose him. Who do you think you are? Do you dare instruct me? [CHÊN *remains kneeling, head bowed. The* DOWAGER *addresses the* EMPEROR.] If you have anything more to say, say it.

EMPEROR [*cowed*]: I have no more to say.

DOWAGER: That's plain enough. [*She addresses* LADY CHÊN.] You've made your petition. Get up!

[LADY CHÊN *stands. She is weeping. She looks at the* EMPEROR *imploringly.*]

EMPEROR [*stammering*]: I – I – I – re – re – gret – I –. [*He now doubles his fists.*] I regret that I – have not finished making our oar. [*His head droops.*] I have failed.

[LADY CHÊN *steps forward, puts her hands around the* EMPEROR's *fists, and the two look at each other with contrition and affection while the* DOWAGER, *watching them, maintains her coolly triumphant smile.*]

CHÊN [*to the* EMPEROR]: The oar can still be made. [LADY CHÊN *turns her head towards the* DOWAGER, *challenging her with a small, curling smile of contempt. She then again addresses the* EMPEROR.] Indeed we have failed. But what about the dowager? Does she think she is actually winning again?

[LADY CHÊN *then loses self-control, first bursting into tears and then breaking into hysterical laughter.*]

DOWAGER: Do you remember where you are? Are we so gay that you can laugh?

CHÊN [*recovering composure and wiping her tears*]: Your maid-slave holds no gaiety in her heart. But she cannot help laughing at the stupidity she observes here.

DOWAGER: And who is stupid?

CHÊN: So the empress dowager actually does think she is winning again? [*They exchange mutually bitter smiles.*] Yes, in a way the empress dowager is winning, but I also think she is losing.

[*Furious, the* DOWAGER *starts to rise from her chair, but* LADY CHÊN, *with a challenging access of will, thrusts out her hand peremptorily and the* DOWAGER, *startled, sinks back into her chair again.* LADY CHÊN *continues to speak rapidly and incisively.*]

CHÊN: The empress dowager knows, actually, that the emperor is a good ruler, that K'ang Yu-wei and the other members of the reform party are men of competence and skill, that the empire has been declining, and that the reforms are our only hope of recovery. But you are not willing to yield power to the emperor, you want to kill competent administrators, you do not care about the future of the empire, you are determined to cancel out the reforms and depose the emperor – because he has acquired some real authority. [*She now addresses the* EMPEROR.] If the empress dowager supported the reforms, our empire would recover prosperity and strength. [*Now again she addresses the* DOWAGER.] Even giving up your control of affairs of state, you could enjoy life there among the hills and waters of the Summer Palace, see all the operas you wish, be comfortable all the rest of your life, and the emperor would protect you. But now the conservatives are winning and, as a result, the empire is weakening, and when the empire is lost, the empress dowager may then not even be able to find a house, let alone a palace, she will no longer enjoy leisure, no longer indulge her whims, playing at sometimes being stern, sometimes generous. Therefore it seems that the empress dowager is actually losing. [*She raises her voice.*] Even though the reforms fail, the emperor need have no regrets. At least he can live with his conscience. But the empress dowager? You have no victory! You cannot live with your conscience!

DOWAGER [*showing some uneasiness but sustaining a formal manner*]: You dare to instruct me, to criticize me to my face!

[*The* EMPEROR *steps forward to intervene, but* LADY CHÊN *gestures to restrain him.*]

CHÊN: I am not insulting you. I only know that my heart aches. Perhaps because Heaven intends an end to our empire, evil spirits have possessed Yüan Shih-k'ai so that he betrays the emperor and helps keep you in power. Open your eyes! On that day when the Great Ch'ing empire falls, it will be by your hands that it is destroyed. Then it will be too late for regrets.

DOWAGER [*moving restlessly in her chair*]: Are you trying to die young?

CHÊN: I am not seeking my death, but I am not afraid of it.

DOWAGER [*pent fury now exploding once more*]: You dare keep on talking! [*She calls.*] Li, come here!

LI [*entering and kneeling*]: Aye?

DOWAGER [*her eyes, fastened on* LI, *imply even more precise instructions*]: This cheap little baggage – throw her out!

CHÊN: Let anyone dare throw me out. I am leaving of my own accord.

[*Calm, erect, and unhurried,* LADY CHÊN *turns and crosses downstage right, passing in front of the* DOWAGER *without looking at her. The* EMPEROR *starts to follow her. She glances back at him but then, putting her hands to her face, goes out quickly, right.* LI LIEN-YING *follows her. The* EMPEROR *shouts at the* DOWAGER.]

EMPEROR: What are you going to do to her?

DOWAGER [*now relaxed and suave*]: Dare I take action against her?

EMPEROR [*still shouting*]: Tell me! Tell me what you are going to do to her!

[*He advances, as though to lay hands on the* DOWAGER, *approaching so precipitately that the* DOWAGER *stands up and retreats a step or two behind her chair. At this point* LI LIEN-YING *re-enters, right, and kneels.*]

LI [*in a stentorian voice*]: Report to Old Buddha, Governor-general Jung-lu has arrived.

[*At this, the* EMPEROR *freezes and then retreats a step or two – and the* DOWAGER *again seats herself.*]

DOWAGER: Have him enter.

LI: Aye!

DOWAGER: We'll wait a bit before deciding how we shall punish that little baggage.

LI: Aye. [*He crosses downstage and then goes out, rear, past the door-screen.*]

EMPEROR [*now in a steadier voice*]: Once more I ask, what are you going to do to her?

DOWAGER: That is my business, not yours. [*The* EMPEROR *is about to retort but then becomes aware that* LI LIEN-YING *and* JUNG-LU *have entered.*] You do not want to see Jung-lu?

JUNG-LU [*kneeling*]: Your slave greets Old Buddha and may fortune be kind. [*He rises and then kneels again, now facing the* EMPEROR.] Your slave greets the emperor, and may fortune be kind. Your slave deserves death.

DOWAGER: He is emperor no longer.

JUNG-LU [*genuinely amazed*]: Old Buddha has already . . .?

DOWAGER: Yes, I have already – deposed him. Didn't Hsü T'ung say yesterday that, to the last emperor of the Sung dynasty, the Chin dynasty awarded the title of Muddleheaded Duke? Muddleheaded Duke suits this one too. [*She addresses the* EMPEROR.] How do you like your title?

EMPEROR: There is nothing more I can say. I only beg you not to be cruel to her.

DOWAGER: Haven't you anything you want to say to Jung-lu? [*She now addresses* JUNG-LU, *with a broad smile.*] Hold onto your head!

JUNG-LU [*kneeling*]: Aye!

EMPEROR [*in a level voice, addressing* JUNG-LU]: I hold no ill will towards you. If we hadn't been driven to desperate measures, I would never have made any move against you. But now that is past, and there's nothing to be said further. I am not concerned about my own life or death. I only hope that you yourself will act in the best interests of the whole nation and not merely add fuel to a smouldering fire.

JUNG-LU: Your slave complies with the imperial command.

EMPEROR: There's nothing more to be said. Get up!

JUNG-LU [*standing*]: Aye.

DOWAGER [*to* JUNG-LU]: But I have more to say to you.

JUNG-LU: Aye.

DOWAGER [*to the* EMPEROR]: But first you step outside until I am ready to deal with you.

EMPEROR: Aye. [*He steps out rapidly, rear, beyond the door-screen.*]

DOWAGER [*to* LI LIEN-YING]: Have them keep an eye on him so he doesn't try running off.

LI [*already moving off beyond the screen*]: Aye!

JUNG-LU: Old Buddha really intends to depose the emperor?

DOWAGER: I'm planning to make Prince Tuan's eldest son the emperor. Do you favour this?

JUNG-LU: Your slave has discussed this matter with the princes and the chief officers. But Sun Chia-nai says that the emperor, as the head of the nation, cannot be so readily deposed.

DOWAGER: Why should old Sun have anything to say about it? He's only a Han-man, a Chinese – and you know I let him in only as a sop to the rest of them.

JUNG-LU: What Old Buddha says is true. But as your humble slave sees it, even though the emperor has failed in proper filial regard for you, he is very popular among the people, especially in the provinces south of the Yangtze, and the people are very enthusiastic about the reforms.

DOWAGER [*irritated*]: When he's already tried to have you killed, why do you now speak up for him?

JUNG-LU: Your slave is not speaking up for the emperor but only observing that, if Old Buddha deposes him, there may be a rising among the people and, if we have a revolt in South China, what will happen next may be more than we want to contemplate.

DOWAGER [*thoughtfully*]: Haven't we any way of dealing with these southern barbarians?

JUNG-LU: We might be able to handle the southern barbarians by themselves, but it won't be so easy to handle the foreign devils.

DOWAGER [*her voice rising*]: Hmph? Have we reached the point where the foreign devils run our domestic affairs?

JUNG-LU: The emperor's reforms are highly regarded by the foreign devils. If they use the deposing of the emperor as an excuse to make trouble for us, we won't be able to handle them easily.

DOWAGER [*frowning*]: Well, granted we must consider this, what course do you suggest we follow?

JUNG-LU: In your slave's humble opinion, it is wiser not to depose the emperor just yet. If you merely compel the emperor to request that Old Buddha resume her control of state affairs, neither the southern barbarians nor the foreign devils can find a pretext for attacking the empress dowager.

DOWAGER [*chuckling*]: Very good, very good! We won't depose him yet awhile. I can take my time – prolong the torture! And we'll see what the southern barbarians and the foreign devils can do about that!

JUNG-LU: Old Buddha is astute.

DOWAGER: And I suppose, in this case, I ought to do the emperor a little favour by allowing some mercy to that little bitch of his, so that people won't go around saying that I killed my daughter-in-law.

JUNG-LU: Right.

DOWAGER [*calling towards the screen*]: You, Li! You, Ts'ui!

LI and TS'UI [*offstage*]: Aye! Aye! [*They emerge at once and kneel.*]

DOWAGER: We'll let that cheap baggage sit around awhile and finish her off slowly.

LI: Isn't this making it too easy for her?

DOWAGER: To let her die now would be easier for her.

LI: Aye.

DOWAGER: For the present I just want to have her locked up. Do you know of some empty, miserable sort of a place where we can pen her in?

LI [*after a brief pause*]: Report to Old Buddha, there is an empty, run-down, old apothecary's shop away off north in the back-third of the palace grounds, the place we call Pei San-so. It's so out-of-the-way that hardly anyone ever goes there and, besides, ghosts haunt it. Your slave suggests that this would do very well.

DOWAGER: Good! Haul her over there and lock her in!

LI: Aye.

DOWAGER [*to* TS'UI YÜ-KUEI]: You take charge of her.

TS'UI: Aye.

DOWAGER [*to* LI LIEN-YING]: I'm putting the emperor in your charge.

LI: Aye!

DOWAGER: Have fifty guards take the emperor to the Ying-t'ai. Since it's the only building on that island in the lake and it's connected by only one bridge, set forty guards there at the bridge and see

that no one crosses that bridge except yourself and the empress.
LI: Aye.
DOWAGER: Have the emperor come in now.
LI: Aye. [LI *remains standing by the screen, indicating by a wave of the hand that* TS'UI *is to carry out the order.* TS'UI *goes out.*]
DOWAGER [*to* JUNG-LU]: What's been done about K'ang Yu-wei?
JUNG-LU: Your slave has sent a telegram to the authorities at Shanghai to have them arrest K'ang Yu-wei when the steamer docks there. He'll be brought back to Peking under arrest.
DOWAGER [*nodding approval*]: Good! I've sent out an order to the chief of the city police to pick up all the other rebels. Don't let any of them get away.
JUNG-LU: They won't get away.
> [TS'UI *re-enters, followed by the* EMPEROR, *who bows towards the* DOWAGER.]
DOWAGER [*to the* EMPEROR]: Because of your failure to show me proper filial respect, I intended to depose you, but at Jung-lu's request, I am granting you pardon for awhile. From today on, however, I shall have you live at Ying-t'ai, and you are not to set foot beyond it except when I send for you. Do you hear?
EMPEROR: Your minister hears.
DOWAGER [*rising*]: Now enough of this. [*She addresses* LI *and* TS'UI.] When you've carried out your assignments, report to me at the Diligent Administration Hall.
LI and TS'UI: Aye! [*Both then call towards the rear.*] Old Buddha is leaving!
VOICES [*off-stage*]: Aye!
> [*The* EMPRESS DOWAGER *rises and walks out at a leisurely pace, followed by* JUNG-LU. LI *and* TS'UI *remain standing at attention in front of the door-screen. Just as the* DOWAGER *is about to step out, she turns a moment and shouts at* LI *and* TS'UI.]
DOWAGER: You fellows keep a sharp eye on them! Mind your duties!
LI and TS'UI [*kneeling*]: Aye. [*The* DOWAGER *has already departed as they reply.* JUNG-LU *goes out close on her heels.*]
LI [*standing up and addressing* TS'UI]: Go attend to Lady Chên.
> [TS'UI *passes the* EMPEROR *downstage without looking at him and goes off right.*]
EMPEROR [*to* LI]: How is Lady Chên?
LI [*slyly*]: She's all right. But the empress dowager is afraid that

COUP D'ÉTAT

Lady Chên is growing tired of the Luminous Benevolence Palace
and is proposing that she take new quarters.

EMPEROR [*irked and anxious*]: What's this?

LI: From today she will reside in Pei San-so.

EMPEROR: Pei San-so?

LI: That's right, the Back-Third, out behind the Bell-Clear Palace.
You've never been there?

EMPEROR: I've never even heard of it.

LI [*blandly*]: Not a bad place. Very quiet during the day, a little
noisy at night.

EMPEROR [*baffled*]: What do you mean, a little noisy at night?

LI [*still bland*]: There's nothing for anyone to go there for during
the day, but ghosts visit there at night.

EMPEROR [*hoarsely*]: Scoundrel! [LI *kneels.*] A place of bad omen!
This is your doing! [*He raises his hand to strike* LI, *but* LI *stands up
and dodges.*]

LI: Your slave would not dare. [LI *and the* EMPEROR *glare at each
other.*]

[Lights out, rapidly.]

SECOND SCENE
Palace of Desolation

Time: June 1, 1899, about 9 p.m.
Place: Pei San-so, in an isolated back section of the Forbidden City.

The moonlit stage shows both the interior of the shack which is now Lady Chên's assigned residence and a small section of the fenced yard in which the shack stands. The yard, at the left, is enclosed by an iron-stake fence topped with barbed wire, the total height about six feet but, along the base, here and there not quite flush with the ground. In the fence there is a gate, fastened with a chain, upstage left. The largest part of the stage, from just left of centre across to the right, shows the interior back and side walls of a high, raftered room, the walls stained at each of the far corners by rain seepage. Moonlight shows through the bracked oiled paper in four small windows high in the rear wall. A narrow doorway in the left wall of the room gives access to the fenced yard. In the right wall of the room another doorway, hung with a stained, torn curtain, leads to the second of the two rooms which now comprise the 'palace' of the emperor's favourite consort.

Within the room a brickstove-bed platform (*k'ang*) occupies the area directly below the high rear windows. On this bed-platform a writing-desk, about two feet high, stands beside a thin pallet. This desk is chipped and battered, as is also the footstool which is placed just in front of the bed-platform. At the far right, upstage, a scarred floorstand holds a potted plant. Downstage left, two formerly handsome but now much patched and chipped chairs stand beside a small tea table. On the wall above the table hangs a picture frame, empty except for a section of cracked glass. Though the walls show the mould of a long-neglected building, the room is otherwise neat and clean.

Though not directly visible, bells are attached both to the door of the shack and to the gate in the fence. These bells sound each time either the door or the gate is opened.

As the curtain rises there is no one in either the half-dark room or the moonlit yard, but somewhere beyond the fence the eunuch, T'ien Kuei-shou, on guard duty as Lady Chên's jailer, sings, off-stage, in a thin falsetto.

T'IEN KUEI-SHOU [*singing, off-stage*]:
   Yang Yen-hui in the palace courtyard
   Sits and sighs, remembering . . .
[*He now approaches, scraping his feet and pounding on the gate so that the bells also sound faintly.*] Hey, you! I brought your food a long while ago! Aren't you ever through eating?
LADY CHÊN [*calling from off-stage right, beyond the curtained doorway*]: I'm through eating.
T'IEN [*visible through the spikes and wire of the fence but remaining outside*]: Put your dishes out then. You're not Lady Chên now!
[*Pushing aside the wadded curtain,* LADY CHÊN *enters the main room. In one hand she carries a lighted candle on a small candle-stick and, in the other, a tray holding several plates and bowls and a pair of chopsticks. As she crosses the room and sets the candle-stick on the table by the lefthand* (outer) *door, light in the room increases. Her face is thin and drawn. She wears a labourer's thin cotton jacket over a purple wadded-cotton gown. Her hair is drawn back and plaited in a single braid. She goes on through the door* (*the bell sounding as she opens it*), *crosses the small yard, and thrusts the tray and its contents through a small opening between the ground and iron fence-spikes to the right of the gate.*]
CHÊN: Here! Take them! [*She shouts, though* T'IEN *is directly outside.*]
[*Moonlight increases and* T'IEN *is visible leaning down outside the fence. He rattles the tray as he picks it up.* LADY CHÊN *has run immediately back inside the house and has flung herself down on the pallet on the platform at the rear of the room. The bell on the house-door still vibrates slightly from the force with which she shut the door as she ran back into the house again.*]
T'IEN [*shouting towards the house*]: Always yelling at me? Who're you trying to scare? Me? Now you're here, why'd you keep on being so cranky? If you had any spunk, you'd have committed suicide.

Whyn't you tie a belt around your neck and hang yourself? That'd settle everything. Hiding there on your bed, I'll bet! That's losing face all right! [CHÊN, *there on the pallet, buries her face in her arms.*] Y'aren't the only one who's having it hard. Here's your old T'ien having it hard along with you, having to keep company with a widow, you might say. You'll never see your husband again! [*Footsteps approach from further off-stage right.*] Hey, who's there?

WANG SHANG [*calling from off-stage*]: It's all right, T'ien. It's just me.

T'IEN: Hey, Chief Wang! I just heard you came back to the palace. It's a good thing it's you and not somebody we don't know.

[*From this point forward,* LADY CHÊN, *inside the house, sits up and, obviously overhearing the conversation, listens attentively.*]

WANG: I got back only three days ago.

T'IEN: What wind blew you out to this shack?

WANG: I had a little free time, and since we used to work together and I heard you were out here, I thought I'd say hello.

T'IEN: More likely you came to say hello to Lady Chên.

WANG [*with an appreciative chuckle*]: You think I have that much time?

T'IEN: Come on now, tell me where you broke loose from.

WANG: The Palace Theatre, where I'm supposed to be attending Old Buddha at the opera.

T'IEN: What's on tonight? Any good?

WANG: First-rate. Chiao T'ien-erh in *The Inquiring Mother*.

T'IEN [*enviously*]: You don't say! What I wouldn't give to hear Chiao T'ien-erh, and in *The Inquiring Mother*! Just my rotten luck, being shunted off here. Unless Old Buddha sends for me, I can't budge. No chance for me to hear any famous actors.

WANG [*smiling*]: If you want to go, it's easy enough. Just go ahead and go. You don't think Lady Chên could actually run off, do you?

T'IEN: Of course not. But if the night watchman comes around and doesn't see me here, I get whipped.

WANG [*still smiling*]: Don't be an idiot. All the watchmen are hanging around the theatre to hear Chiao T'ien-erh.

T'IEN: Don't kid me.

WANG: Who's kidding you? Go on and go. I'll see you later. I'm going to look up Hsiao-te Chang. [*Exit.*]

T'IEN: Hey, wait! We'll go together.

[*As the footsteps of* WANG *and* T'IEN *fade away,* CHÊN *peers through a slit in one of the paper windowpanes as though assuring herself of their departure. She then comes downstage, talking to herself.*]

CHÊN: Wang Shang! The emperor's servant, and my servant! Since the empress dowager dismissed him, how has he managed to come back? [*An owl hoots outside. Terror-struck,* CHÊN *looks about nervously, pacing the room.*] I can't stand it here! I can't bear it any longer! For nine whole months [*counting on her fingers*] I haven't seen the emperor, and they say he's sick, too. [*Her voice rises to a wail.*] And I can't go to see him. [*There is a knock at the gate.*] Who is it? [*She screams.*] Who is it?

WANG [*softly*]: Your slave, Wang Shang.

CHÊN [*going towards the door*]: What is it?

WANG: An important matter to report to Lady Chên.

[CHÊN *steps cautiously outside the house, but seeing* WANG'*s face, beyond the fence, made somewhat grotesque by shadows from the barbed wire in the moonlight, she draws back.*]

CHÊN [*in a choked voice*]: You aren't – a ghost?

WANG: Do not be alarmed, my lady. Your slave, even if he were a ghost, wouldn't come to frighten you.

CHÊN: Weren't you here a moment ago?

WANG: Yes, I had to get T'ien out of the way somehow. [*As* CHÊN *takes courage and approached the fence,* WANG *continues in a whisper.*] The emperor may be arriving here soon.

CHÊN: The emperor! Here?

WANG: The emperor, yes. Here. And your slave has the key to this gate. If you are willing, your slave will now open the gate, come in, and explain everything.

CHÊN [*now with animation*]: But how did you get the key?

WANG [*holding up a chain of keys*]: Your slave is now working in the Imperial Treasury office. These are master-keys.

CHÊN [*impressed*]: Well, really! Open the gate, then. Quickly.

WANG: Good.

[CHÊN *retreats towards the house as* WANG *busies himself opening a series of padlocks. He follows* CHÊN *into the house and kneels.*]

WANG: May fortune be kind, my lady.

CHÊN: Get up now. Tell me, how did you get yourself into the Imperial Treasury?

WANG: When, because of last September, Old Buddha threw your slave out of the palace, your slave still kept on looking for ways to serve the emperor. Among the other fellows of course I have many old friends, and so I kept in touch. Just before New Year's, through Chief T'ang who works for the empress dowager, I managed to present some money and a few other gifts to Li Lien-ying and flattered him by asking him to accept me as foster-son. So just a few days ago Li persuaded the empress dowager to give me this small post in the Treasury.

CHÊN: I see. But you say the emperor is coming. How could His Majesty possibly come here?

WANG: By good luck. [*They both hear footsteps and* WANG *hurries out.*] Let me see who's coming. [*He goes through the outer gate and addresses someone off-stage.*] Is the emperor coming?

BOY'S VOICE [*off-stage*]: He is coming!

WANG [*rushing back into the house*]: Permit me to report to my lady, the emperor is coming!

[*Eager but bewildered,* CHÊN *paces about, brushing at her hair, smoothing her dress.*]

CHÊN: Go welcome him! Go out and welcome him!

WANG: Aye. [*Exit.*]

CHÊN: How can I face him when I look like this?

[*Lifting the candle, she tries to see herself in the reflection from the broken glass in the picture frame. As footsteps approach again, she jerks off the shabby jacket and flings it inside the curtained door at the right. Her purple wadded-cotton gown, though severe, is not unattractive. Meanwhile, outside,* WANG *stands at the open gate, and the* EMPEROR *strides through.* CHÊN, *who has once more picked up the candle, is setting it on the table as the* EMPEROR *bursts in. She kneels.*]

CHÊN: Your maid-slave reverently greets Your Majesty.

[*The* EMPEROR, *wearing civilian dress, looks old and weary. He seizes her hand.*]

EMPEROR: Get up now. [*He leads her closer to the candle.*] Let me have a good look at you.

[*They gaze at each other, not speaking. Then* CHÊN *looks down at her hands. The* EMPEROR *examines them, smoothing them. Still holding her hands, he swings about the room. He drops her hands for a moment as he peers into the inner room through the right-hand doorway. At this point* CHÊN *wipes away tears with her sleeve. The* EMPEROR *re-emerges from the inner room.*]

EMPEROR: This place is hell! How can you stand such a place? [*He calls.*] Wang Shang!

WANG [*entering*]: Aye.

EMPEROR: Look here! Is this any place for a human being?

WANG: Your slave knows that it is not.

EMPEROR: Can't you find someone to fix this place up?

WANG: The fellow on duty here is a natural-born king of hell. But in a while now I may manage to work Li Lien-ying around to assigning a couple of honest fellows in T'ien's place. Then maybe I can fix things up a bit here.

EMPEROR: Good. You know that Lady Chên is more important to me than anyone. I'd rather risk more suffering myself than have her put up with this place in the state it's in now.

WANG: Your slave understands.

EMPEROR: That's all.

WANG: Aye. [*Exit.*]

CHÊN: Your Majesty has recovered from his illness?

EMPEROR [*with a sigh, harassed*]: It wasn't, in a manner of speaking, an illness. They tried to poison me, put something in my food that made me sick after every meal. With several months of this, I was finally more dead than alive. [*His voice drops.*] Just before New Year's I really thought I would not survive long enough to see you again.

CHÊN [*tonelessly, as still dazed*]: They told me Your Majesty was very, very ill. I wanted to come to Ying-t'ai to see you, but they would not let me out of here.

EMPEROR: At least the provincial governors and other leading men began to speculate about the 'illness', sent telegrams inquiring about my health – and newspapers in the south ran articles and editorials saying sharp things about the empress dowager. And this public pressure seems finally to have made the poisoners desist. That's why I'm now gradually recovering.

CHÊN: But Your Majesty is still very thin, and your face has no colour.

EMPEROR: But you are much thinner too. [*He takes her hands again.*] My poor dear little one. In all your life you could not even have dreamed of such suffering. [*He caresses her hands.*] These lovely nails of yours, all so broken now.

CHÊN [*withdrawing her hands*]: But how did Your Majesty manage to come here?

EMPEROR: Wang Shang's loyalty is our good fortune. The moment he got himself back into the palace, just three days ago, he started figuring out a way for me to come over here. Tonight he sent wine from the Imperial Treasury over to Ying-t'ai, and all my guards are drunk. He also had one of the boy-eunuchs who is specially devoted to me acquire these clothes and slipped him across the lake with a boat on a ferry-rope so he could pull us back to the shore without a sound. Then, by roundabout paths, the youngster led me here. I could never have found this place by myself.

CHÊN: Wang's loyalty is truly our good fortune.

EMPEROR: Alas, he's about all we have left. Nearly all the good men of the reform party have been killed or exiled, and all servants loyal to me have been thrown out of the palace. K'ang Yu-wei and Liang Ch'i-ch'ao have escaped and are safely out of the country.

CHÊN: They tell me Jung-lu is now both Grand Councillor and Minister of War.

EMPEROR: Jung-lu has always been the empress dowager's teeth and claws. And I don't blame him too much. I'm more disturbed that our despicable Yüan Shih-k'ai still flourishes. They tell me the empress dowager has now appointed him governor of Shantung.

CHÊN: That turncoat, for all his cunning, will come to no good end.

EMPEROR: When I gave him that golden arrow, he took that oath before me and Heaven, calling on Heaven to bring down upon him if he broke his trust, death-dealing anxieties and misfortunes.

CHÊN: Your maid-slave ventures the opinion that such a death will still come upon him.

EMPEROR [heavily]: Nonetheless, because of him all our carefully prepared reforms are already destroyed.

CHÊN: Why is Your Majesty still so disturbed about all this now?

EMPEROR: Now the dowager has gone beyond merely a hatred of reforms and is taking up the line of Prince Tuan, Kang-i, and all the other notorious diehards, keeping all Chinese out of office and loathing all foreigners. She's ordered the training of militia in the provinces, actually expecting such a lot of bumblers to be able to stand up against the armed forces of the foreign nations.

CHÊN: Isn't this just talk and daydreams?

EMPEROR: On the contrary. By her own hands and by her own acts the Ch'ing dynasty will fall – and soon.

CHÊN: Emperor!

EMPEROR: Now she's about to depose me and give the title of emperor to Ta-ah-ko. To me personally this does not matter, but it's one more signal towards the fall of the dynasty. What's the use of a puppet emperor? Better if I had died long ago. [*Seizing* CHÊN'*s hands again, he speaks with increasing intensity.*] I'm not just bemoaning myself. I made up my mind quite awhile back to end all this, to make away with myself. But I also made up my mind that first I must see you again. I've been looking to find a way. Now I am here. Now there is nothing more to . . .
[*While the* EMPEROR *has been talking,* CHÊN *has been staring up at the rafters. Suddenly she points towards them.*]

CHÊN: Look!

EMPEROR: What?

CHÊN: A snake!

EMPEROR [*lunging up towards the rafters and flailing with his arms*]: Get out! Get out!

CHÊN [*rigid as the snake begins to slither along a crossbeam*]: Aiya!
[*At* CHÊN'*s scream,* WANG SHANG *rushes in. The snake, meanwhile, having dropped to the floor – grazing* CHÊN'*s shoulder as it descends – glides under the curtain into the back room (right). The* EMPEROR, *having flung a chair after it, has now caught up* CHÊN *in his arms.*]

EMPEROR [*to* WANG]: Snake! There in the back room. Go after it. Kill it.

WANG [*seizing the footstool as a weapon and plunging through the curtained doorway*]: Aye! [*The* EMPEROR *and* CHÊN *start to follow him, but* WANG *re-emerges almost at once.*] Report to Your Majesty, it's gone out the window. It's out there in the grass.

EMPEROR: Let it go, then.

WANG [*kneeling*]: Aye. And I now remind Your Majesty that it's coming on time for the second nightwatch. The watchmen and T'ien Kuei-shou will be arriving. May I request that Your Majesty now make his departure – quickly.

EMPEROR: You're right. I must go.

WANG: Aye! [*Exit.*]

EMPEROR [*picking up the chair and seating* CHÊN]: Shocking! That you should be here in a den of snakes.

CHÊN: The ground is low and damp here. There are not only snakes but mice and rats – and the hawks swoop down. In the night there are noises – knocking, coughing, noises like something or someone breaking in here. But now I am used to all this. At first I used to wake up in the dark and nearly die of terror.

EMPEROR: How can you keep on living, here in this hell?

CHÊN [*weeping*]: The choice is not mine. As long as Your Majesty lives, I shall try to keep on living too.

EMPEROR: You suffer, and it is I who cause this suffering.

CHÊN: It is not Your Majesty who makes me suffer. But I don't want to die. I can't die. I'm young. I do not want to die. I hate death.

EMPEROR [*tenderly*]: My little one. My own little one.

CHÊN: But ever since last September, life is only misery. Now you've seen this place, but there's much you haven't seen – and no time now to tell you: the foul meals, all cold, rotten table-leavings, and the jeers and jawings of that T'ien Kuei-shou, calling me *idot* and *empty mud-belly*, and *deadhead*. And if I say anything back, he sneers at me, saying I'm no great lady here. [*She sobs.*]

EMPEROR: That filthy good-for-nothing. How dare he?

CHÊN: And when I was sick, they wouldn't send a doctor, wouldn't let me have any medicine. Nobody did anything.

EMPEROR [*commiserating*]: Ah, ah, such a life. For my own little one.

CHÊN: All the same, if you'll live, one more day or many days, I'll keep myself alive too. I'll suffer rather than die. I'll let that T'ien creature sneer at me for being a coward, not daring to commit suicide. I'll keep on living because I still have faith in you.

EMPEROR [*affectionately*]: What hope do you have – in me?

CHÊN: I can hope that your day will still come.

EMPEROR [*sadly*]: Could you think I would not hope for this too? But now I am no more than a common prisoner, a puppet. I see nothing ahead but one closed road after another and then death. What more can I say?

CHÊN [*standing up*]: Emperor, your future is not a closed road. You are not yet thirty, and the empress dowager is already sixty-five. She isn't likely to live to be a hundred. Endure for another eight or ten years, and then Your Majesty will at last hold real power.

EMPEROR [*with a trace of reviving animation*]: Another eight or ten years?

[*From a distance comes the sound of the rattle, signal of the approaching second nightwatch*: dee-dee, da-da, ta-ta, dee-dee, da-da, ta-ta.]

CHÊN: If Your Majesty will only be patient, if you will take care of your health . . .

EMPEROR: Eight or ten years? But I am not sure I can hold out even through this year.

CHÊN: Does Your Majesty mean to say that he cannot endure suffering, even for just a few more years?

[WANG SHANG *enters and kneels.*]

EMPEROR: What is it?

WANG: May I remind Your Majesty that, in not more than a very few minutes now, the watchmen will be here at the gate.

EMPEROR: Just one second more.

WANG: Your slave is not afraid to lose his life. But if Your Majesty is found here, Your Majesty will never be able to come here again. And the empress dowager will be even more harsh with Lady Chên.

EMPEROR: You're right. I'll leave at once.

WANG: Aye.

CHÊN [*desperately*]: For the nation? For me? Can't you hold out for a few years more?

[*The watchman's rattle sounds again.*]

EMPEROR [*bracing himself*]: Then – for you, for the nation, I must keep on living.

CHÊN [*taking his hands*]: And for Your Majesty's sake, I can then keep on living too.

[*The watchman's rattle sounds once more.*]

EMPEROR: Not just ten years, but twenty, thirty, a hundred. Still we can wait!

[*They step out into the yard. As they stop near the gate and smile at each other, the boy-eunuch,* LIU SAN-ERH, *appears just beyond the fence, together with* WANG SHANG.]

LIU [*in a harsh whisper*]: The watchman! He's almost here!

WANG [*entering the gate and kneeling*]: Emperor! You must leave!

EMPEROR [*to* CHÊN]: Now I must go.

CHÊN: Until next time.

EMPEROR [*as he goes through the gate*]: Until next time. [*He suddenly turns and raising his arms, as though poling a boat, calls out softly.*] Our oar!

CHÊN [*also raising her arms, as if poling*]: Our oar!

[*The* EMPEROR *and* LIU *disappear through the dark.* WANG *locks the gate and also departs.* CHÊN, *running into the house, steps up onto the* k'ang *and peers through the paper slits in the rear window. She leans against the wall and again raises her arms as though poling a boat. Heavy approaching footsteps and the sound of the watchman's rattle reverberate through the whole area.*]

[Curtain.]

ぷ ACT IV

FIRST SCENE

The Inspection of the Palace

Time: July 16, 1900 about 7 p.m.
Place: the Pei San-so shack (as in Act III, Second Scene).

Now, in Pei San-so, the yard beyond the shack is in complete darkness. Inside the shack the room is basically as before. However, flourishing potted plants now stand here and there, new cushions brighten the bed and the chairs, and the tattered windowpanes have been replaced with fresh new paper.

In the distance the sound of gunfire is punctuated by occasional artillery bursts, reverberations from the battle in Peking around the Legation Quarter, to which Tung Fu-hsiang's Kansu soldiers and the Boxers are laying siege.

A knock at the outside door (left) brings Lady Chên from the inner room. As she opens the door, beyond which there now seeps a mist of very dim moonlight, the boy, Liu San-erh enters, carrying a tray of fruit and small cakes.

LIU: May fortune be kind, my lady.

CHÊN [*accepting the tray and placing it on the writing-desk*]: But I've just had dinner. Why do you bring more?

LIU: Wang Shang sends these privately and offers his compliments.

CHÊN: Ever since Wang had you assigned here, I'm supplied from morning to night with good things. I am much in your debt.

LIU: It is nothing, really. But now your slave can also report that His Majesty will be arriving here very shortly.

CHÊN: Good. And now, what other news today?

LIU: They say it's touch-and-go at Tientsin, that the foreign troops are already at the city gates.

135

CHÊN: What about the Boxers and Tung Fu-hsiang's troops? At the Legation Quarter? What's going on there?

LIU: Who knows? Every day they claim they're about to take over, but it's been nearly a month now and no sign of surrender.

CHÊN: Ever since dinner I've been hearing gunfire and the artillery again. I thought the fight must still be going on.

LIU: At least out here you're far away. Up close the noise is terrible.

CHÊN: How could Old Buddha be so stupid, letting those Boxers come inside the city?

LIU: But what can we do now? Except for the Legation Quarters, the Boxers now control the whole of Peking. They've stuck up altars everywhere, they're always burning incense and worshipping the spirits and worshipping their leaders like god-spirits too – and they swagger around in turbans and those red sashes of theirs wrapped around their bellies, and they've got swords and guns and just cut down or shoot anyone they happen to feel like killing. They set fire to houses too. What don't they do? But they have Prince Tuan and Kang-i and other high officials backing them, so what can we do about it?

[*Hearing footsteps,* LIU *now dashes outside. Meanwhile, from below the bed-platform,* CHÊN *takes out a toy boat, modelled on a Pearl River skiff, with small silk figures of a man and a woman. From the toy boat* CHÊN *takes a toy wooden oar and thrusts it into her belt. During this action the following conversation is audible between an attendant and* LIU *conversing near the fence in the dark.*]

LIU [*by the gate*]: Who's there?

ATTENDANT'S VOICE [*beyond the fence*]: Just me, San-erh.

LIU: Is the emperor on his way here?

ATTENDANT'S VOICE: He'll be here in a moment now. Wang Shang sent me on ahead just to be sure no one else is around.

LIU: No one's here.

[*At this point,* CHÊN, *who has been overhearing through the doorway, slides the toy boat under the writing-desk and then brushes her dress with her hand.*]

ATTENDANT'S VOICE: I'll greet the emperor in front of the gate here.

LIU: Good. [*He re-enters the house.*] Report to my lady, the emperor is now arriving.

CHÊN: Good. Please greet him outside the door.

LIU: Aye.

[*As* LIU *steps out, leaving the door wide open, light from a gauze lantern glimmers through the yard and* WANG SHANG, *passing* LIU, *enters the room.*]

WANG [*kneeling*]: May fortune be kind, my lady, I report, His Majesty has arrived.

CHÊN: Good! [*Sound of footsteps outside.*]

LIU [*outside the door*]: May fortune be kind, Emperor.

[*The* EMPEROR *enters. His face is drawn and anxious, but he appears in somewhat better health than in Act III.* CHÊN *and* WANG *kneel.*]

CHÊN: May fortune be kind, Your Majesty. [WANG *bows and goes out.*]

EMPEROR [*extending his hand*]: Come, get up. [*They seat themselves at the table.*]

CHÊN: Your maid-slave hears that the situation in Tientsin is touch-and-go.

EMPEROR: No longer touch-and-go. Gone. Tientsin has fallen to the foreign troops.

CHÊN: Lost? Tientsin?

EMPEROR: Gone! Lost! Fallen! And do you know that Prince Tuan, Kang-i, and all those other bigots are still insisting that the empress dowager not allow any peace negotiations? Prince Tuan is going around saying that we lost Tientsin to the foreigners only because the Boxers didn't pray hard enough, weren't pious enough, and that the loss is only temporary – and he keeps announcing that the Boxers' defence of Peking is so mighty that the foreign devils can never break through. He's not only a lunatic but beyond curing.

CHÊN: But does the empress dowager literally believe what he says?

EMPEROR: For a while she didn't seem to be paying much attention to him. Then Jung-lu told her that it was Lien Wen-chung, an Assistant Grand Councillor, who contrived to persuade the foreign diplomatic corps into sending that demand that she hand over the control of state affairs to Jung-lu. And Jung-lu told her it was Prince Tuan who put Lien Wen-chung up to it.

CHÊN: Contrived? I see! Prince Tuan knew it would put her in a fury to be told to hand over her power and she'd promptly declare war on all the foreigners.

EMPEROR: Exactly! But after the dowager heard from Jung-lu that

Prince Tuan was behind that demand, she had a blazing row with Prince Tuan and told him, 'If foreign troops enter Peking, I'll have your head chopped off.'

CHÊN: Well, in that case, the dowager is going to allow the peace negotiations after all.

EMPEROR: Oh, no! She'll threaten Prince Tuan, but she hasn't the least intention of opening negotiations with the foreigners. She's just as much of a lunatic as Prince Tuan. She also thoroughly believes that the foreigners can be wiped out by those Boxers.

CHÊN [*thoughtfully*]: I used to think, despite everything, that the dowager had real ability and insight, that she could be decisive, that she knew how to size up people. But it seems she's not really that clever after all or she wouldn't be swallowing all this nonsense of Prince Tuan's and actually believe in this magic the Boxers preach. It looks to me as though she really hasn't come to any decision and actually doesn't know what to do.

EMPEROR [*nodding agreement*]: She's getting old, and she's confused. But she still can handle Prince Tuan and the other diehards.

CHÊN: Tientsin's lost – and the Boxers still haven't captured the legations. At least this means that Prince Tuan and the rest of them won't be making any move against you right now. But if they did, do you actually think the dowager could still control them?

EMPEROR: Don't forget that Prince Tuan has ambitions. If, as he hopes, his son Ta-ah-ko is made emperor, then, since Ta-ah-ko is still only a half-grown boy, Prince Tuan will be named regent.

CHÊN: But if it hadn't been for Liu K'un-i holding out against it, the dowager would have made Ta-ah-ko emperor some months back.

EMPEROR: You don't suppose for a minute that the dowager is afraid of Liu K'un-i? She's still shrewd enough to realize that, if she deposes me, the southern provinces will rebel.

CHÊN: Well, anyhow, Ta-ah-ko isn't emperor yet. He's so arrogant himself, and with Prince Tuan's even worse arrogance, to have Ta-ah-ko be emperor would be intolerable.

EMPEROR: Ta-ah-ko never refers to me as *emperor* but as *that student of the foreign devils*.

CHÊN [*with irony*]: Someday he may find he'll have to be the student of this foreign devils' student.

EMPEROR: We'd best not hope for that. Do you know that, a few mornings ago, around six in the morning, Prince Tuan himself, along with Prince Chuang and some of the others, went out themselves with fifty or sixty Boxers chasing what they call the *second-string hairy men*? That's their name for anyone who's become a Christian or has adopted any Western customs or has any Western-style education. The whole gang of them actually pounded on the doors of my own palace and milled around there all morning yelling for me as a *second-string hairy man* and demanding that I come out to them.

CHÊN: Not really!

EMPEROR: Yes, really. There was Prince Tuan himself out there, jumping up and down like a wild man, cursing me, and all his Boxers yowling and leaping with him. It was all such a racket that I nearly lost my temper.

CHÊN: Was Old Buddha behind this?

EMPEROR: Not at all. When she found out, she gave Prince Tuan a terrific tongue-lashing and had Jung-lu round up that particular mob of Boxers. The whole lot of them had their heads chopped off, at her orders, and Prince Tuan had to kowtow to her and beg for mercy to save his own head.

CHÊN: In that case, why didn't Jung-lu take such an ideal chance to get her to order the Boxers disbanded entirely?

EMPEROR: It's not all that simple. You see, just before that, when she'd already sent an order to the Kansu soldiers and the Boxers to stop trying to capture the legations and when that order had been in effect for less than twenty-four hours, Yü-lu presented her with that premature telegram claiming that the foreign armies had been driven from Tientsin – and she began believing all over again that the Boxers have magic power after all.

CHÊN: But now the foreigners have captured Tientsin. Won't this wake her up?

EMPEROR: The news has upset her, but not enough to shake her out of her faith in magic, not even though the authorities in the southern provinces have now refused to send troops and the only troops we have for the defence of Peking is this same Peiyang army that's just taken a beating at Tientsin. It's my guess that, within another month, we'll see the fall of Peking also.

CHÊN: Suppose the foreign armies do fight their way into Peking? What do you think the dowager will do?

EMPEROR: Arrange to kill herself probably.

CHÊN: No, I don't think so. She'll try to save herself, she'll run off. She won't care what happens to Peking.

EMPEROR: I can't imagine she'd do that.

CHÊN: You can't? Even forty years ago, wasn't she already the one who insisted on fighting it out with the foreigners? But when the Anglo-French armies marched into Peking, what did she do? She ran off to Jehol. She's a gambler, I think, likes to take long chances for the adventure of it. But behind that hard face of hers, she's fundamentally a coward. I'm sure she'll run away again.

EMPEROR: Perhaps.

CHÊN: And what does Your Majesty plan to do? Will you run off along with her, or will you stay here?

EMPEROR: It's – hard to know till the time comes.

CHÊN: Would you be ready to stay here and take the care of the nation wholly on your own shoulders?

EMPEROR: If it were just myself, don't you think I would stay here? But [*he looks away from* CHÊN *and down at the floor*] if the empress dowager should compel me to leave, then . . .

CHÊN: I see. Your Majesty has still not made up his mind.

EMPEROR [*with a sharp intake of breath*]: I must make up my mind.

CHÊN: Does Your Majesty remember about the small boat your maid-slave has so often mentioned?

EMPEROR: The small boat? Do you think I could forget it?

CHÊN: Would you like to see this small boat?

EMPEROR [*puzzled*]: Why, yes – I certainly – would.

> [CHÊN *steps quickly up to the bed-platform, brings the boat from under the writing-desk, and sets it on the table in front of the emperor.*]

CHÊN: Is this our little boat?

EMPEROR [*examining it with obvious pleasure*]: Beautiful! But where does it come from?

CHÊN: I made it myself.

EMPEROR: You made it yourself?

CHÊN: Yes, I made it myself. I had Liu San-erh find me some wood – and since I have nothing to do all day, I whittled along on it slowly. Now, here it is – the little boat.

EMPEROR: Remarkable! Delightful!

CHÊN [*resuming momentarily the child-like tone and manners of years earlier, and pointing to one of the dolls on the boat*]: That's you!

EMPEROR [*taking up the same tone*]: Then who's this?

CHÊN: You know.

EMPEROR [*with a boyish smile*]: That is you and this is I. We two, husband and wife, are riding in this little boat.

CHÊN [*promptly*]: In *our* little boat.

EMPEROR: In *our* little boat. But now who's imagining things?

CHÊN [*pointing*]: Do you notice – the pair of verses written here? [*The* EMPEROR *holds the boat close under the candle and, tracing the minute script with his finger, attempts to read it.*]

EMPEROR: What's this word, the one below *prince*?

CHÊN: *Rides.* Rides or *buffets* waves. You know, when there's a heavy wind.

EMPEROR: Now let me try again. *Prince. Rides, buffets. Wave Wind.* I see now! The prince buffets waves and winds. [*He moves his finger down the second line.*] *Wife.* What's this word after *wife*?

CHÊN: *Recalls.* From years long past.

EMPEROR: That's it. The wife recalls. *Water. West River.* Now we have it. *The prince fights on through waves and winds. His wife recalls West River, those calm waters.* [*Still holding the boat, he gathers both* CHÊN'*s hands with his free hand. His voice warms with approval and excitement.*] The boat is a wonderfully skilful piece of work, but these verses are even more skilful.

CHÊN: Perhaps so. But don't you notice anything missing?

EMPEROR [*placing the boat carefully on the table*]: The oar?

CHÊN: Are you still remembering that we can also make an oar?

EMPEROR [*his eyes fixed on the toy boat*]: But our oar was broken even before we had finished working on it.

CHÊN: But wouldn't you consider trying to make another one?

EMPEROR [*he has been running his hand along the edge of the boat, but now looks up abruptly, his fingers tensed*]: You mean you want me to make up my mind to stay here, not to leave Peking?

CHÊN [*earnestly*]: If you will stay here, if you will not run away, this will be your Heaven-sent opportunity. [*She speaks slowly and with emphasis.*] But if you run off along with the dowager, you will still be a puppet, no matter where you go – and, worse than that, there'll be no responsible chief of state here in Peking, the city will be in turmoil, and the whole nation is likely to collapse soon after.

EMPEROR: But if I don't run away, what then?

CHÊN: If Your Majesty will stay here in Peking, you can rule the nation and sustain the dynasty. When the foreign armies enter the city, you can send your officials to the commander, negotiate a truce, and sign a treaty. The foreigners know who you are, the emperor who introduced reforms, the ruler who has no connections with the Boxers. With you they will be willing to negotiate. And when all the people and the governors of the provinces learn that you now hold power again and are their defence against disaster, they will acclaim you and support you. This will make you even more powerful, increase your prestige so much that the foreign powers will not dare to make unreasonable demands. Peking will be saved from complete destruction, the nation will be preserved, and you will have all the powers of state firmly in your own hands.

EMPEROR [*meditating*]: But the foreigners don't like us, and they can be brutal.

CHÊN: In your maid-slave's opinion, the foreigners are human beings, and I think they will respect the usual laws for dealings among nations.

EMPEROR: But if they decide to be brutes, what then?

[*Footsteps resound outside.*]

CHÊN: Then you may lose your life. But then at least you would be dying for your country. You would at least meet death with honour.

[WANG SHANG *bursts in and kneels.*]

EMPEROR [*seeming not to notice* WANG *and still addressing* CHÊN]: Well, I . . .

WANG [*interrupting*]: Your Majesty! Old Buddha is coming!

EMPEROR [*appalled*]: No! Then I must leave!

[*The noise of chair-carriers, shouts, and footsteps penetrates the house.*]

WANG: We had no warning. I'm afraid that's Old Buddha herself, right there outside the gate.

EMPEROR: What shall I do?

CHÊN: In there. Go into the inside room.

EMPEROR: Well – I suppose I must.

[*Followed by* CHÊN, *the* EMPEROR *disappears through the curtained doorway, right.* WANG *hurries out into the yard, which is still dark.*

THE INSPECTION OF THE PALACE

He locks the door to the house. Inside the house, CHÊN *returns to the main room and stands by the door, listening. Through the general roar of voices beyond the fence comes the sound of the fence-gate opening and the voices of* WANG *and* LIU SAN-ERH *just outside the house-door.*]

WANG and LIU [*together*]: May fortune be kind, Old Buddha. May fortune be kind, Empress.

[*Through the next several interchanges the yard still remains in total darkness and the voices come out of the dark.*]

DOWAGER: Aren't you Wang Shang?

WANG: Aye, your slave.

DOWAGER: A fine, loyal slave! Aren't you waiting here for your master?

WANG: Your slave would not dare.

DOWAGER: Open this door! I'll attend to you later.

WANG [*addressing* LIU SAN-ERH]: Open the door at once.

LIU: Aye!

[*Inside the house* LADY CHÊN *moves as though to open the door, but then, her eye falling upon the toy boat, she seizes it and thrusts it under the writing-desk. The* DOWAGER *enters.* CHÊN *kneels.*]

CHÊN: May fortune be kind, Empress Dowager.

[*The* EMPRESS *and* LI LIEN-YING *now enter.* CHÊN, *who has just risen from her knees, bows slightly to the* EMPRESS.]

CHÊN: May fortune be kind, Empress.

DOWAGER: I've come to ask you where the emperor is.

CHÊN [*outwardly calm*]: Your slave does not know.

DOWAGER: You don't know? Very strange. Directly after dinner he came to the Peaceful Long Life Palace, but then he vanished. I sent someone to look for him at Ying-t'ai, but he was not there either. [*Her tone is heavily ironic.*] He wouldn't come here would he?

CHÊN: He has not come here.

DOWAGER: But I have already received reports that he was seen coming here.

CHÊN: Your maid-slave knows nothing of this. Perhaps whoever made the report mistook what he saw.

DOWAGER [*with her mocking smile*]: So you know nothing of this. I'm going to search this place.

[*The* DOWAGER *starts towards the inside room, but* CHÊN *steps adroitly in front of the doorway.*]

CHÊN: This is your maid-slave's sleeping-room, a poor, cramped, dusty place. The Empress Dowager may suffer some damage to her gown, going in there.

DOWAGER: Get out of the way!

[*Just as the* DOWAGER *reaches for the curtain,* LI LIEN-YING *steps forward and kneels.*]

LI: Old Buddha, this place really is a dirty hovel. Let your slave step in and search for the emperor.

DOWAGER: Very well. But make a thorough search.

LI [*already shoving aside the curtain*]: Aye!

[*Meanwhile, the* EMPRESS *has been examining the main room, has spotted the toy boat under the writing-desk, has pulled it out, and now shows it to the* DOWAGER.]

EMPRESS: Old Buddha, look at this!

DOWAGER: What's that to look at? [*She is impatient and scornful.*] Put it back where you got it.

[LI LIEN-YING *re-emerges and kneels.*]

LI: Report to Old Buddha, your slave has searched the room thoroughly.

DOWAGER: Well? Have you found someone?

LI: Your slave has made a thorough search. He has searched the bed and the bedcovers, examined everything, but the emperor . . .

DOWAGER: The emperor – what?

LI: The emperor is not there.

DOWAGER [*taken aback*]: Well! Well, that's that!

EMPRESS [*still holding the toy boat*]: Old Buddha, look at these verses.

DOWAGER: Verses?

EMPRESS [*pointing to the lines written on the toy boat cabin*]: Here they are.

[*The* DOWAGER *takes the boat, carries it to the light of the candle on the table, squints, and reads.*]

DOWAGER: *Prince. Waves. Winds. Wife. West River.*

EMPRESS: The composer is rather pretentious.

DOWAGER [*to* CHÊN]: *Prince,* I imagine, signifies the emperor? The verse means that Chên the concubine wants him to take advantage of a fortunate wind, right?

CHÊN: Right.

DOWAGER: So *wife,* in the second line, no doubt means you. *Wife* thinks of *West River.* So I suppose that even the waters of the West River couldn't wash away your humiliation, but you're scheming for the day when the emperor has a fair wind and makes his way through the waves to good fortune. Then you'll take your revenge against me. Right?

CHÊN: The line only means that your maid-slave remembers the little boats she watched on the Pearl River when she was young. Nothing else is implied.

DOWAGER: So you dare lie to me? Or you mean to suggest that I am not able to understand literary allusions? [*She addresses the* EMPRESS]: Is my interpretation correct or not?

EMPRESS: She would be glad enough if you and I would both drown in the West River.

LI: Appalling! If a flood should submerge the Dragon King's temple, what would become of your slave in such a disaster?

DOWAGER [*to* LI]: I'll look into this further. Who gave her materials to make a boat? Summon Wang Shang.

LI [*shouting towards the door*]: Summon Wang Shang!

VOICE [*offstage*]: Aye!

[WANG *enters at once and kneels.*]

WANG: Old Buddha, may . . .

DOWAGER [*holding the boat and tapping it*]: The materials for making this? You doubtless presented them to Lady Chên as a mark of your loyalty and reliability? Right?

WANG [*his eyes fixed on* LI]: Your slave would not dare.

LI: Report to Old Buddha. Although Wang Shang once served the emperor, your slave observed that this Wang is honest and has good principles and so, some time ago, adopted him as his son. Furthermore, Wang Shang is not employed here but in the Imperial Treasury. Consequently, he would not dare to offer any gift to Lady Chên.

DOWAGER [*to* WANG]: Well then, what did you come here for?

WANG: Your slave dares not say.

DOWAGER: Never mind that. Say it.

WANG: The emperor . . .

DOWAGER: The emperor what?

LI [*exchanging glances with* WANG]: Where is the emperor?

WANG: The emperor . . .

LI: Do you mean to say that the emperor has escaped? Say it!

WANG: Aye. The emperor – has escaped.

[*In accord with their individual temperaments and concerns, the* DOW-

AGER, *the* EMPRESS, *and* LADY CHÊN *all show amazement and shock.*]

DOWAGER [*recovering outward composure*]: He has escaped?

WANG: When your slave was returning to the Imperial Treasury office, he saw the emperor some distance off, wearing ordinary streetclothes and hurrying north.

DOWAGER: He's gone to the north?

LI: Now your slave understands. Only three days ago the emperor was inquiring how long it takes to go by carriage from the palace to the Marco Polo bridge.

DOWAGER: That's what he asked? And you saw him headed north?

WANG: Your slave would not dare give a false report. Since the emperor is neither here nor at Ying-t'ai, he must have run off.

DOWAGER [*to* CHÊN]: You did not know he intended to run off?

CHÊN: Your maid-slave did not know.

DOWAGER: Hmph! We'll see how far he can run. [*She addresses* LI LIEN-YING.] Have Jung-lu send out troops, cavalry, to find the emperor and bring him back.

LI: Aye. But if the emperor is unwilling to return, what then?

DOWAGER [*stonily*]: Then tell Jung-lu – to do as he sees fit and – I will not blame him.

LI: Aye.

DOWAGER: You will also have further search made of the palace grounds, all the palaces, make sure the emperor is not lurking here somewhere.

LI: Aye.

DOWAGER [*handing him the toy boat*]: And take this curiosity out and have it burned.

LI: Aye. [*He takes the boat, opens the door, and stands in the doorway addressing attendants in the dark yard.*] Ts'ui, convey to Jung-lu the verbal order of Old Buddha to send out cavalry to search for, locate, and capture the emperor. Tell Jung-lu that, if the emperor refuses to return, Jung-lu may proceed as he sees fit. Also, set up a search for the emperor throughout the palaces and the palace grounds. And here [*he hands the boat to someone beyond the doorway*], Old Buddha commands that this toy boat is to be smashed and burned. [LI *now turns, facing into the room, but the house-door remains open.*]

DOWAGER [*to* CHÊN, *fiercely*]: If he doesn't return, you need not plan to live long.

[*Beyond the doorway there is the sound of splitting wood, a flash of flame, and then a steady flicker of fire.*]

LI: Old Buddha, would you like to watch the burning of the boat?

DOWAGER: Good. And order the sedan-chair.

LI [*shouting*]: Bring up the sedan-chair!

[LI *escorts the* DOWAGER *through the door, and the* EMPRESS, *with a broad sneer directed at* CHÊN, *at once follows.* CHÊN, *expressionless, is on her knees, her arms crossed. Outside there is talk and jostling. Reflection of the fire and shadows of people moving appear not only through the doorway and in the glow of fire in the yard, but also through the paper windowpanes. There is a crackling and small explosion and heavy drift of smoke, at which point the* DOWAGER'S *party, again in darkness, goes out through the fence-gate,* CHÊN *stumbles off into the inner room, and* WANG SHANG *appears, standing alone, in the house-door. A moment later* LI LIEN-YING *appears beside him.*]

LI: Well now, you're a bold one all right. Even daring to hide the emperor right here, of all places. If I hadn't had my wits about me, you and I would be missing our heads by now. [*He slaps* WANG *across the mouth.*] I've got to go tend to the sedan-chair, but I'll tend to you all in good time.

[LI *goes out. After seeming to contemplate the curtain in the doorway to the inner room with close attention,* WANG *then turns and departs also. At this point* LADY CHÊN *and the* EMPEROR, *with his arm around her, emerge from the inner room. His face and hers are both tear-stained, and she is still sobbing, her head on his shoulder.* WANG *re-enters, carrying a few chips of charred wood which the emperor, still holding* CHÊN, *reaches for with his free hand.*]

EMPEROR [*softly*]: They have burned our boat.

WANG: It's a shame. Nothing left but those splinters. [*He goes out.*]

EMPEROR [*crushing the small chips in his hand*]: A while ago I couldn't make up my mind. Now my mind is made up.

CHÊN [*suddenly alert*]: What is Your Majesty's decision?

EMPEROR: I have decided not to leave.

CHÊN [*embracing him*]: If Your Majesty will not run away, even at the risk of death, your maid-slave will stay beside you.

EMPEROR: Death, if death comes. But we'll not run away.

CHÊN: Die, if we must. But we'll not run away.

[Curtain.]

SECOND SCENE
The Death Pledge

Time: August 15, 1900, about 3 a.m.
Place: Courtyard of the Peaceful Long Life Palace.

In the centre of this outer courtyard of the Peaceful Long Life Palace, the palace of the empress dowager, stands a watchmen's yardhouse with porch and stone steps. There is a large tree in the area between the house and a section of wall to the left marking an inner compound. There is a gate in the wall. The gate stands open and through it a section of a wellsweep is visible. Farther upstage left, a gate into a cross-section of wall gives access to the palace. Even further upstage left an areaway between walls leads to the Sought-for Long Life Hall. In the opposite wall of the outer compound, to the right, a jar-shaped gate, downstage right, opens to a road outside the palace area.

Except for dim light from lamps hanging above the gates, the courtyard is dark. The whole area vibrates with ear-splitting artillery fire from the allied armies bombarding Peking. In pauses between artillery bursts, sounds as of heavy furniture being dragged about, and confused shouting, indicate that the empress dowager and her entourage are preparing to flee.

Two eunuchs and one of the palace girls, disguised in non-descript streetclothes and carrying parcels of stolen valuables, creep warily along the passage between the lefthand wall and the house – which stands dark and empty – and skitter across the courtyard and on out through the righthand gate. In the darkness far within the areaway between the walls there are shots and shouts and groans. Two more eunuchs dash through and out the righthand gate. One of them clutches his wounded arm. Then the eunuch Ch'i appears through the palace gate. He carries a lighted lantern. He shouts upstage towards the dark areaway leading to the hall in the rear.

CH'I: Old Buddha wants to know who's running off and what all that noise is over there.

TS'UI YÜ-KUEI [*speaking from somewhere in the back areaway*]: What's that? What's Old Buddha want?

CH'I: Who's running off? What's all the noise?

TS'UI [*now visible, gun in hand, coming along the passage*]: Just some rascals grabbing stuff and making off. The gun squad finished off one of them and captured six. They're up there now, crawling on their knees and yowling for their lives.

CH'I: Very soon now the empress dowager will be coming out, to start on her journey. If you let anymore of those rascals go scuttling through here, she'll give us even more trouble.

TS'UI: T'ang Kuan-erh has forty men guarding the Following Harmony Gate. We've got a patrol at the Nourishing Harmony Pavilion. I've got a squad of forty up here at the Long Life Hall. But patrols or no patrols, all the no-account eunuchs and palace girls are scrambling to get out of here, and just pulling authority on them doesn't work any more. So what can we do?

CH'I: Well, steer them off in some other direction. Just don't let them go scrambling through here. We can't use any more rumpus around here just now.

[CH'I *goes back through the gate and* TS'UI *appears about to follow him. He pauses for a moment, however, muttering to himself.*]

TS'UI: With all these foreign soldiers right at the walls of Peking, what I wouldn't give just to run away too. If we don't let these eunuchs and palace-girls sneak out, there's nothing for it but to shoot them down, every one of them.

[*Shooting breaks out again in the areaway.* TS'UI *flattens himself against the wall just as* T'IEN KUEI-SHOU, *his arm full of loot, comes running out of the passage.* TS'UI *stops him at gunpoint.*]

T'IEN [*howling and dropping his bundles.*]: No! No! Chief Ts'ui, don't shoot!

TS'UI: You son of a turtle, do you want to keep on living?

[*Two squadmen now emerge behind* T'IEN, *swing past him, and block his possible escape across the courtyard.*]

T'IEN: I won't run away. Don't shoot!

TS'UI [*to the squadmen*]: Haul him off up there and shoot him.

SQUADMEN: Aye! [*They seize* T'IEN.]

T'IEN [*screaming and sobbing*]: Let me live!

SQUADMEN [*yanking him*]: Come on, you!

T'IEN [*as he and the squadmen disappear back into the dark of the rear areaway*]: Mercy! I won't run off now!

> [TS'UI *starts to cross the courtyard, downstage, when he hears footsteps outside the gate to the right, stops by the stone steps of the yardhouse, and raises his gun.*]

TS'UI: Who's there?

> [HSIAO-TE CHANG, *carrying a hurricane lantern, comes through the gate.*]

HSIAO: Just me, Ts'ui. Put down that gun.

TS'UI: How could I know it was you? Are the carriages ready?

HSIAO: The whole city's run off in a panic. Where am I going to find carriages? I finally managed to get together three mule carts. But the streets are so mobbed, it took next to forever just to get those three carts from Righteous Victory Gate over here. I'm all of a sweat. But the carts are out there.

> [CH'I *enters, from the left.*]

CH'I: Have you brought enough carts and carriages?

HSIAO: All I could lay hands on. Three mule carts.

CH'I: Old Buddha wants to know.

HSIAO: Would you just as soon tell her for me?

CH'I: All right. I'll tell her. [*He goes out again, left.*]

HSIAO: Has the emperor come? [*He swats his arm and brushes off a mosquito.*]

TS'UI: Chief Li's gone over to Ying-t'ai to get him. He hasn't come so far.

HSIAO [*ominously*]: We'd better start now or it'll be too late.

TS'UI: What's the situation outside? Have the foreign troops broken through to the inner city yet?

HSIAO: Already in the eastern section, I hear.

TS'UI: Already!

HSIAO: Actually there doesn't seem to be much fighting. Wherever things get too rough, the Kansu soldiers and the Boxers just drop everything and run off. And there are deserters everywhere, from all the units, Central Guards, Tiger Hunt Troops, Sharpshooters, Peking Field Forces. Their officers can't control them anymore.

TS'UI: What about the leaders, the Boxers' Senior Master and Junior Master?

HSIAO: Those two hid out long ago. Nobody knows where they are. Yesterday Prince Tuan, Prince Chuang, Kang-i, and lots of others went looking for those two everywhere and couldn't find either one of them.

TS'UI: They're the ones who cosied Old Buddha into thinking that they could hold off the foreign devils. But now, when things get hot, they crawl off somewhere. [*Rifle shots from the palace gunsquad sound again from the rear areaway.* TS'UI *looks back up the passage, turns, stamps his feet.*] It's those Boxers who ought to be shot. They're the devils.

[TS'UI *sets off at a run up the passageway.* CH'I *comes in once more, left.*]

CH'I: Ts'ui? Where's Ts'ui gone off to?

HSIAO: He's gone up there, to the Hall.

CH'I: Old Buddha told him to send somebody to fetch Lady Chên from Pei San-so. Where is she? It's been a long while.

HSIAO: Is Old Buddha going to take her along?

CH'I: Who knows? Old Buddha just says that when Lady Chên comes, she's to wait out here.

HSIAO: Wait out here? What does that mean? [HSIAO *swats another mosquito.*] Why's she want her to wait out here? Curse these mosquitoes. Listen to that one buzz! [*He slaps himself again.*]

CH'I: It's because of that well in there. [*He indicates with a jerk of his head the open gate (downstage left) through which the wellsweep is visible.*] That's where the mosquitoes come from.

HSIAO [*fretting*]: Well, all I hope is that Old Buddha doesn't start another row here, at this point. I hope she'll wait until we're all well on the way to Shensi before she does anything more about Lady Chên.

CH'I: She does as she pleases. Why should you worry?

HSIAO: Why should I worry. After all the trouble I've had to get hold of those three carts? And it's already the fifth watch? And the sun'll be up any moment now, and if she doesn't get away practically this minute, most likely it's I that'll have to go jump in that well.

[TS'UI YÜ-KUEI *reappears, coming down the passage.*]

TS'UI: Lady Chên is coming.

CH'I: Well, tell her to wait out here. I'll report to Old Buddha. [*He goes out, left.*]

TS'UI: Has the emperor come?

HSIAO: Haven't heard anything about him.

[*Guided by the boy eunuch,* LIU, LADY CHÊN *comes down through the passage. She wears formal palace garb, as in the days before Pei San-so, and moves with dignity.* TS'UI *and* HSIAO *bow casually, slightly bending one knee.* LIU *bows and retreats, rear.*]

CHÊN: Is the empress dowager still inside?

TS'UI: Old Buddha says Lady Chên is to wait here.

CHÊN [*obviously uneasy*]: Oh? The empress dowager wants me to wait here?

[*Two boy eunuchs appear through the palace gate. They carry a large chair and a yellow satin cushion. Mounting the steps of the yardhouse, they arrange the chair and cushion on the porch and then depart, again through the same gate.*]

TS'UI: Old Buddha says she'll see you out here.

CHÊN: I've heard that the foreign troops are already inside the city, and that the empress dowager is fleeing. Is this true?

TS'UI: That's not for me to say. Better ask Old Buddha.

CHÊN: A long while ago I said I thought she would run off.

[*The* EMPRESS DOWAGER *emerges from the lefthand gate. She is followed by the* EMPRESS, LADY CHIN, *and the eunuchs* CH'I *and* LIU SAN-ERH. *The eunuch* HSIAO, *who has been standing by the left corner of the yardhouse swings into the procession with the other eunuchs. The* DOWAGER *wears a flowered cotton gown and her hair is dressed in the fashion of a Chinese peasant woman. With great formality she ascends the yardhouse steps and seats herself in the yellow-cushioned chair. The* EMPRESS, LADY CHIN, *and the eunuch* CH'I *range themselves on the steps as a token court.* HSIAO *and* LIU, *now at either side of* LADY CHÊN, *kneel with her at the foot of the steps.* TS'UI *stands guard between the yardhouse and the passageway.*]

CHÊN: May fortune be kind, Old Buddha.

HSIAO and LIU: May fortune be kind, Old Buddha.

DOWAGER [*addressing* HSIAO]: You collected the wagons?

HSIAO: Aye.

DOWAGER: Why did you bring only three?

HSIAO: Old Buddha cannot imagine how many thousands of people are fleeing, crowding and blocking the streets. Every wagon in the city of Peking is already in use.

DOWAGER: What's the situation now?

HSIAO: Foreign troops have already penetrated everywhere, burning, plundering, killing. I've seen them with my own eyes. I beg Old Buddha to start at once.

DOWAGER: Hmph! If you saw the foreign soldiers with your own eyes, you would have been killed out there too. Are you going to give me any more of that nonsense?

HSIAO [kowtowing]: Your slave would not dare. Your slave has not seen any of the foreign soldiers.

DOWAGER: Now – what's the situation? Let's have the truth this time.

HSIAO: Except for so many people trying to get out of the city and everybody in a panic, it's not yet too bad. There are rumours that the foreign troops are already inside the city, but the reports may not be accurate.

DOWAGER: Very well. You may go.

HSIAO: Aye. [HSIAO goes out, right.]

DOWAGER [pointing now individually to everyone present except LADY CHÊN and TS'UI YÜ-KUEI]: You, all of you, go inside now. [They go out left, back through the gate into the palace. She now addresses TS'UI.] Why isn't the emperor here?

TS'UI: Chief Li went over to Ying-t'ai after him, and that was a long while ago. They should be here very soon.

[Shouts rise from the rear hall, followed by an agonized scream.]

DOWAGER: Tell the squadmen to drag those people off somewhere where I can't hear them.

TS'UI: Aye. [He goes out, rear, through the passageway.]

DOWAGER: Get up! Talk!

CHÊN [standing]: As you say.

DOWAGER: Now you are pleased. The foreign devils have arrived. [She indicates her flowered cotton gown.] Never before have I had to humiliate myself like this, dressing like this. Aren't you going to laugh at me?

CHÊN: I may deduce that this means you are about to run away, just as, forty years ago, you ran off to Jehol?

DOWAGER [annoyed but controlling herself]: No need to talk about that now. I'd already planned, four or five days ago, to go out of the city for awhile, but there's been all this difficulty about locating carriages and wagons – and besides, the emperor has been sick.

CHÊN [*surprised and suspicious*]: The emperor has been sick?

DOWAGER: Yes, sick. He told me he would not leave, no matter what.

CHÊN [*relieved*]: Oh.

DOWAGER: That's what ails him, that he doesn't want to leave. That's why I've asked you to come attend to him.

CHÊN: You want your maid-slave to attend to him?

DOWAGER: If you can cure this sickness of his, I will overlook your past offences, and mother-in-law and daughter-in-law can leave here together, along with him. But [*with a leer*] if you don't want to leave, and then the foreign devils do what they please with you, don't blame me.

CHÊN [*curtly*]: Your maid-slave will not hold you to blame.

DOWAGER: Are you actually not afraid of the foreign devils?

CHÊN: I am not afraid of them. Your slave knows that the emperor is not afraid of them either.

DOWAGER [*probing*]: It seems that you are sure the emperor will not go away.

CHÊN: What is more, it is your maid-slave who has persuaded [*she emphasizes this*] the emperor not to go away.

DOWAGER [*with cool malice*]: Since you were able to persuade him not to go away, can't you also persuade him that he must go away with us?

CHÊN: Your maid-slave refuses to persuade the emperor to remain a puppet.

DOWAGER [*glowering*]: Instead, you want him to stay here and play the slave to the foreign devils?

CHÊN: This slave is simply hoping that the emperor will sustain his responsibility for the empress dowager. That is all.

DOWAGER: That is all? His responsibility for me?

CHÊN: Since the empress dowager brought our nation to its present crisis, isn't it the emperor's first responsibility, for your sake, to resolve the crisis?

DOWAGER [*now in a fury*]: Hmph! I was going to persuade you to accompany us, to accompany the emperor. And here you are mocking me again. Tell me, don't you want to keep on living?

CHÊN: Why should I wish to die?

DOWAGER: If you want to keep on living, persuade the emperor to leave with us. Remember that you cannot defend yourself.
CHÊN: The empress dowager threatens me with death. The empress dowager supposes that I am afraid to die.
DOWAGER: You dare start an argument with me? You are not afraid to die? This makes me want to put you to death.
CHÊN [*calmly*]: I am afraid the empress dowager will not have the triumph she hopes for. Two years ago the empress dowager took the powers of state into her own hands again and cancelled the reforms. She thought that she had triumphed, but I told her then that she had failed – and now she sees my words fulfilled. If the empress dowager had any conscience, any courage, she would be defending the capital and herself fighting to the death. Those she should be putting to death are Prince Tuan, Kang-i, and all the other bigots. It is you, the empress dowager, who should be negotiating now for peace. Instead you are afraid. You want me to encourage the emperor to run away along with you. As usual, you hope to settle everything by not settling anything. Do you want to be a failure again? Do you want to be a woman without a country?
[*During this challenge from* CHÊN *the dowager shows conflicting moods, her fury at war with her fears; but her fury against* CHÊN *finally gains ascendancy.*]
DOWAGER: I want to know the bitterness of a woman without a country! I want to know the bitterness of death! [*She shouts now.*] You there! You fellow, Ch'i! Come here!
CH'I [*from beyond the wall*]: Aye! [*Accompanied by two boy eunuchs,* CH'I *enters through the lefthand gate.*]
DOWAGER [*pointing*]: Take a good grip on her and throw her into the well.
CH'I and BOYS: Aye.
[CHÊN *stands quietly. Neither* CH'I *nor the boys make any move towards her.*]
DOWAGER [*standing*]: You snivellers! [*She comes down the steps.*] Must I heave her up and throw her in myself?
[*Artillery fire resumes, now much closer.* TS'UI YÜ-KUEI *comes from the rear hall, running.*]
TS'UI: Report to Old Buddha, the foreign soldiers will be here, right here, very soon. Prince Tuan, Prince Ch'ing, Prince Na, Prince Su, Kang-i, and the others are all outside, waiting for you.

Ma Yü-k'un has brought up a regiment of one thousand to escort you on your journey. Will Old Buddha please start the journey – now?

DOWAGER [*now showing agitation*]: All right. All right. Tell the empress and Lady Chin and the rest to come out and get into the wagons. I'll come in a moment.

TS'UI: Aye. [*He goes through the lefthand gate.*]

DOWAGER [*addressing* CH'I]: You stay here. I'll send the girls off first.

CH'I and BOYS: Aye.

[*The* DOWAGER *mounts the steps and seats herself again. The* EMPRESS, LADY CHIN, *and several attendants come through the lefthand gate, closely followed by* TS'UI.]

DOWAGER [*addressing them*]: The empress and Lady Chin will now go out to the wagons. You others go back inside and wait for me.

THE EMPRESS and LADY CHIN: Aye.

[*With* TS'UI *escorting them, the* EMPRESS *and* LADY CHIN – *who gives an anxious glance at* LADY CHÊN – *go out the righthand gate, from which* TS'UI *then returns and retires with the other attendants, through the lefthand gate.* CH'I *and the boys continue to stand beside* LADY CHÊN. *Just as the attendants disappear through the gate,* LI LIEN-YING, *a suit of ordinary streetclothes slung over his arm, comes running down through the rear passage.*]

LI [*kneeling*]: The emperor is coming. Because the emperor insisted on going to Pei San-so first, we were delayed.

DOWAGER [*increasingly distraught*]: You there, Ch'i! Take Lady Chên back up there to the Hall for the present.

CH'I and BOYS: Aye.

[*They look at* LADY CHÊN *inquiringly. She answers their glances with a slight smile and then walks ahead of them. She stumbles slightly, puts her hand to her belt, and then goes on, followed by* CH'I *and the boys, down the rear passageway.*]

DOWAGER: Bring the emperor here!

LI: Aye. But [*he holds up the streetclothes he is carrying*] may I report to Old Buddha that the emperor emphatically refuses to put on these ordinary streetclothes.

DOWAGER: You go bring him out here immediately.

LI: Aye.

[LI *goes off through the lefthand gate. The* DOWAGER *resettles herself uneasily in her chair and mops her face with a large*

handkerchief. She is staring into space and shows a start when the
EMPEROR, *who has opened the lefthand gate softly and crossed to*
the foot of the steps, kneels and addresses her.]
EMPEROR: May fortune be kind, Venerable Parent.
DOWAGER: Get up! [*The* EMPEROR *stands.*] The foreign troops will
soon be reaching the palaces. You must leave.
EMPEROR: Where is Lady Chên?
DOWAGER: Never mind about her. Get on out there to the wagons,
quickly.
EMPEROR: Your minister has been to Pei San-so to look for her.
She's not there, and she doesn't seem to be here either. I've been
asking everyone, and no one will give me a clear answer. Venerable
Parent, what have you done with her?
DOWAGER: Wasn't she the one who persuaded you not to leave?
EMPEROR [*startled*]: How does the Venerable Parent know this?
DOWAGER: There is a powerful spirit who tells me everything. She
persuaded you not to leave, but, since she fears death, she was
anxious to get away. She has gone on ahead.
EMPEROR: This your minister refuses to believe.
DOWAGER [*coolly*]: People have been saying you are stupid, but this
I had refused to believe. Now, however, I see that you are both
stupid and a lunatic.
EMPEROR: She hasn't run away. She would never run away.
DOWAGER: Well, never mind what I say. You can wait here for her.
I'm leaving.
[*Artillery fire comes with thunderous bursts. Moving with formal*
rigidity but clearly terrified, the DOWAGER *stands and comes down*
the steps.]
EMPEROR [*face to face with her*]: Now! You tell me where she is!
DOWAGER: Haven't I already told you?
EMPEROR: But your minister knows that she could not, would not,
run away.
DOWAGER: If you don't believe me, go on out there and see what
you find in the wagons.
[*The* EMPEROR *stares incredulously at the* DOWAGER. *She stares*
back. He drops his eyes, takes a few steps, his eyes downcast, stops,
picks up something from the left side of the stone steps. It is the
toy oar.]
EMPEROR: Our oar! She dropped it. How could she?

DOWAGER: Hurrying to get away, of course. She was afraid she wouldn't get out of here in time.

EMPEROR: I still will not believe that she would break her pledge to me.

DOWAGER [*slyly*]: Are you sure she broke her pledge? If I hadn't given her my promise, she wouldn't have been willing to go.

EMPEROR: What did you promise?

DOWAGER: She told me not to leave. She told me to have Prince Tuan and Kang-i killed. She told me to give you the powers of state again so that you could save us from shame.

EMPEROR: Venerable Parent, you are trying to delude me.

DOWAGER: Why should I be deluding anyone at this terrible moment?

EMPEROR: Venerable Parent? You are trying to lure me into going out to the wagons?

DOWAGER: I swear that, if I am trying to lure you, my grave will be dug by strangers.

EMPEROR: Well then, I suppose . . .

DOWAGER: It's up to you whether or not you choose to believe me.
[*There is a further thunder of artillery.*]

EMPEROR: Then she is already out there in the wagons? Is she?

DOWAGER: With all this noise, can we wait any longer? Let her worry about you out there in the wagons. Get along, quickly.

EMPEROR: Your minister goes at once.
[LI LIEN-YING, *who has been lingering in the shadows of the passageway, steps forward. The* DOWAGER *exchanges, with* LI, *an amused smile. The* EMPEROR *has his head bowed and is turning over the toy oar in his hand.*]

DOWAGER [*to* LI]: Give every attention to the emperor. Take him out to the wagons.

LI [*with a grin which the* EMPEROR *does not observe*]: Aye.
[*The* EMPEROR *and* LI *exit right. The* DOWAGER *stands watching the gate even after it closes behind them.* TS'UI YÜ-KUEI *now steps out through the lefthand gate and the* DOWAGER *turns, obviously expecting him to be there.*]

DOWAGER [*to* TS'UI]: You there! Have them bring that cheap baggage back down here now.
[TS'UI *merely signals with his hand, indicating that* CH'I *and* LADY CHÊN *are within the shadows of the passage. When* CHÊN *emerges, her face shows anger and contempt.*]

TS'UI: At your command.

DOWAGER [*to* CHÊN]: Now we do not need you to take care of any more persuading.

CHÊN [*indicating* TS'UI *and* CH'I]: They've told me, you slanderer, you vicious . . . Lies and lies! What I might have expected. But [*her voice is bitter*], that the emperor could let you trap him again, that he believes you, believes I would break the promise we made. [*More artillery bursts, now ear-shattering.*]

DOWAGER [*cowering at the noise, but shouting full voice*]: Now! Now! [*She charges towards* TS'UI, CH'I *and the boys.*] Are you going to obey me?

CH'I *and* BOYS: Aye. [*They approach* LADY CHÊN, *but still make no move to touch her.*]

TS'UI [*shouting*]: You chickenheads! Get out of the way! I'll do it myself!

[TS'UI *rushes at* LADY CHÊN, *but, just as he is about to seize her wrists, he is taken aback by* CHÊN'S *steady gaze and drops his hands.*]

CHÊN [*to* TS'UI]: You are not privileged to lay hands on me. You do not need to touch me. I will take myself there. [*She walks towards the gate opening into the wellyard, but, before entering the gate, stops, turns, and calls out.*] Your Majesty, I am still here! Come back!

[*At this moment a flute tune sounds from within the wellyard, the tune first heard in Act II.* TS'UI, CH'I *and the boys kneel at the gate which* CHÊN *has now entered. The* DOWAGER *abruptly mounts the porch steps again, as half in retreat and still curious for a better view. Through the sound of the flute comes a dull, muffled splash. Immediately a file of eunuchs moves out through the wellyard gate. They kneel, like automata, before the* DOWAGER. *At a further burst of artillery fire, the* DOWAGER *edges backward up two more steps and stands, visibly trembling, in front of her chair.*]

DOWAGER: Heaven . . .

TS'UI [*standing by the wellyard gate*]: Report to Old Buddha, Lady Chên has entered Heaven.

DOWAGER: Now we – go.

[*Sound of commotion outside the righthand gate is punctuated by the voice of the* EMPEROR, *shouting.*]

EMPEROR [*still outside the gate*]: Let go! Let go of me!